UKRAINIAN PICTURE DICTIONARY COLORING BOOK

Over 1500 Ukrainian Words and Phrases for Creative & Visual Learners of All Ages

Color and Learn

Lingo Mastery

ISBN-13: 978-1-951949-65-5

Free Book Reveals the 6-Step Blueprint That Took Students **from Language Learners to Fluent in 3 Months**

- **6 Unbelievable Hacks** that will accelerate your learning curve
- **Mind Training:** why memorizing vocabulary is easy
- **One Hack to Rule Them All:** This <u>secret nugget</u> will blow you away...

Head over to **LingoMastery.com/hacks** and claim your free book now!

CONTENTS

INTRODUCTION

This **Ukrainian Picture Dictionary Coloring Book** is a fun vocabulary building tool with illustrations that you can color while studying. It covers an immense range of topics that will help you learn everything related to the Ukrainian language for everyday subjects, from family members and animals, to body parts and job descriptions.

This introduction is a guide to help you get started with Ukrainian and polish your basic grammar, spelling, punctuation, and vocabulary skills. Good luck—and **most importantly, enjoy yourself!**

BASICS OF THE UKRAINIAN LANGUAGE

I.   Reading and pronunciation rules

a.   Vowels

There are ten letters in the Ukrainian language that are used as vowels: А, Е, И, І, О, У (**simple vowels**) and Є, Ї, Ю, Я (**iotized, or "soft" vowels**).

Let's see how they are pronounced and represented in transcription in this book. The first six vowels are quite simple:

Letter/pronunciation	Example
Aa – [a] - like 'a' in 'car'.	ананас – [a-na-NAS] – *pineapple* але – [a-LE] – *but*
Ee – [e] - like 'e' in 'letter'.	дерево – [DE-re-vo] – *tree* небо – [NE-bo] – *sky*

Ии – [y] - like 'y' in 'sympathy'.	син – [syn] – *son*
Ii – [i] - like 'i' in 'bit'.	i – [i] – *and*
Оо – [o] - like 'o' in 'dog '.	олівець – [o-li-VETS'] – *pencil* око – [O-ko] – *eye*
Уу – [u] - like 'oo' in 'tooth'.	луна – [lu-NA] – *moon* друг – [druh] – *friend*

Iotized (soft) vowels (Є, Ї, Ю, Я)

Letter/pronunciation	Example
Єє – [йє] - like 'ye' in 'yes'.	Європа – [yev-RO-pa] – *Europe*
Її – [йі] - like 'ye' in 'yeast'.	їжа – [YI-zha] – *food*
Юю – [йу] - like 'you' in 'youth'.	юнак – [yu-NAK] – *young man*
Яя – [йа] - like 'ya' in 'yard'.	яблуко – [YAB-lu-ko] – *apple*

There are different pronunciations, depending on the position of the iotized vowel:

- at the beginning of the word:

їсти – [YIS-ty] – *to eat*

юрист – [yu-RYST] – *lawyer*

язик – [ya-ZYK] – *tongue*

- in other cases, typically in the middle of the word. The ionized vowels in this position make the preceding consonant sound soft:

малюнок – [ma-L'U-nok] – *drawing*

тисяча – [ty-S'A-cha] – *thousand*

b. Consonants

Familiarize yourself with these phonetic phenomena before studying consonants.

1) Voicing and devoicing

Unlike Russian (and some other Slavic languages), the Ukrainian language doesn't have voiceless consonants. Consonants do not change at the end of a word. For example, 'd' at the end of a word is still pronounced like a 'd', not as a 't'.

2) Soft and hard consonants

Depending on their 'neighbors', Ukrainian consonants can sound either hard or soft. Most consonants can be both hard and soft, while some of them are always hard or always soft.

Consonants that can be both hard and soft

Б	В	Г	Д	З	К	Л	М	Н	П	Р	С	Т	Ф	Х
Б'	В'	Г'	Д'	З'	К'	Л'	М'	Н'	П'	Р'	С'	Т'	Ф'	Х'

The ionized vowels (Є, Ї, Ю, Я) make consonants sound soft.

Of course, **letter 'ь' or soft sign** has the same effect on preceding consonants. In other cases these consonants sound hard.

The letter 'ь' will be represented in transcription by means of a single quotation mark(').

The following consonants are always hard, regardless of the vowel that follows:
Жж, Шш, Цц

The following consonants are always soft, regardless of the vowel that follows:
Чч, Щщ, Йй
So we won't be using the **single quotation mark** ['] with them to indicate softness.

Ukrainian consonants

Letter/pronunciation	Example
Бб – **[b]**, like 'b' in 'bear'.	бабця – [BAB-ts'a] – *grandma*
Вв – **[v]**, like 'v' in 'vest'.	ваза – [VA-za] – *vase*
Гг – **[h]**, like 'h' in 'hoody'.	гарно – [HAR-no] – *beautiful*
Ґґ – **[g]**, like 'g' in 'get'.	ґудзик – [GUD-zyk] - *button*
Дд – **[d]**, like 'd' in 'do'.	дуб – [dub] – *oak*
Жж – **[zh]**, this sound is a bit special. To understand how to pronounce it, say 'pleasure' or 'measure'. Now pay attention how you pronounce the letter 's' in these two words. The consonant you get is [zh].	жінка – [ZHIN-ka] – *woman*
Зз – **[z]**, like 'z' in 'zoo'.	зуб – [zub] – *tooth*
Йй – **[j]**, like 'y' in 'yoga'.	музей – [mu-ZEJ] – *museum*
Кк – **[k]**, like 'k' in 'sky'.	мак – [mak] – *poppy*
Лл – **[l]**, like 'l' in 'lemon', but with your tongue on the teeth and not on the palate like in English.	лампа – [LAM-pa] – *lamp*
Мм – **[m]**, like 'm' in 'milk'.	мати – [MA-ty] – *mother*
Нн – **[n]**, like 'n' in 'net'.	один – [o-DYN] – *one*
Пп – **[p]**, like 'p' in 'spoon'.	папір – [pa-PIR] – *paper*

Рр – [r], like 'r' in 'sorry'.	рука – [ru-KA] – *hand*
Сс – [s], like 's' in 'small'.	сік – [sik] – *juice*
Тт – [t], like 't' in 'step'.	тигр – [tyhr] – *tiger*
Фф – [f], like [f] in 'film', just a bit more relaxed.	фото – [FO-to] – *photo*
Хх – [kh], like 'h' in 'home'.	хліб – [khlib] – *bread*
Цц – [ts], like the combination of [t] and [s] sounds.	це – [tse] – *this*
Чч – [ch], like 'ch' in 'chicken'.	час – [chas] – *time*
Шш – [sh], like 'sh' in 'shy'.	школа – [SHKO-la] – *schools*
Щщ – [sch], like the combination of [s] and [ch] sounds.	щит – [schyt] – *shield*
ь – has no sound, just makes the preceding consonant soft. It is never capitalized.	низький – [nyz'-KYJ] – *low*

There are two consonant combinations that actually stand for one sound:

дж – **[dzh]**, like 'j' in 'jam'.	бджола – [bdzho-LA] – *bee*
дз – **[dz]**, like 'ds' in 'friends'.	дзеркало – [DZER-ka-lo] – *mirror*

There are certain words that begin with 'у' and have an alternate form that begins with 'в':

у мене / в мене

у же / вже

у дома / вдома

The form that begins with 'у' is used after words ending in consonants:

Він **у**же тут.

Він **у**дома.

The form that begins with 'в' is used after words ending in vowels:

Вона **в**же тут.

Вона **в**дома.

The adverbs 'також' і 'теж' are often interchangeable.

II. Grammar

Ukrainian grammar is rather intense, since the relationship between words is expressed through endings. Pronouns, nouns, adjectives, and verbs change their endings depending on the grammatical category, and the patterns for these changes require lots of knowledge and practice.

Since grammar is not the major focus of this book, this section includes only basic aspects, such as what grammatical categories mean and what forms different parts of speech can take. We'll learn more precisely how to build these forms in other books.

a. Pronouns

Categories of pronouns:

- Person (1st, 2nd, 3rd)
- Number (singular and plural)
- Case (see the table below)
- Gender (only for 3rd person singular)

Cases of personal pronouns

Nominative	Genitive	Dative	Accusative	Instrumental	Locative
Я – I 1st person singular	Мене	Мені	Мене	Мною	Мені
Ти – You 2nd person singular	Тебе	Тобі	Тебе	Тобою	Тобі
Ми – We 1st person plural	Нас	Нам	Нас	Нами	Нас
Ви – You 2nd person plural	Вас	Вам	Вас	Вами	Вас
Він – He 3rd person singular masculine	Його	Йому	Його	Ним	Ньому
Вона – She 3rd person singular feminine	Її	Їй	Її	Нею	Ній
Воно – It 3rd person singular neutral	Його	Йому	Його	Ним	Ньому
Вони– They 3rd person plural	Їх	Їм	Їх	Ними	Них

Possessive pronouns

Personal pronoun	Possessive pronoun
я – I	мій – my/mine
ти – you	твій – your/yours
ми – we	наш – our/ours
ви – you	ваш – your/yours
він – he	його – his
вона – she	її – her/hers
воно – it	його – its
вони – they	їх – their

Possessive pronouns and their gender, number, and cases

Gender / Number	Nominative	Genitive	Dative	Accusative Animate	Accusative Inanimate	Instrumental	Locative
Masculine Singular	Мій	Мого	Моєму	Мого	Мій	Моїм	Моєму
	Твій	Твого	Твоєму	Твого	Твій	Твоїм	Твоєму
	Наш	Нашого	Нашому	Нашого	Наш	Нашим	Нашому
	Ваш	Вашого	Вашому	Вашого	Ваш	Вашим	Вашому
Feminine Singular	Моя	Моєї	Моїй	Мою		Моєю	Моїй
	Твоя	Твоєї	Твоїй	Твою		Твоєю	Твоїй
	Наша	Нашої	Нашій	Нашу		Нашою	Нашій
	Ваша	Вашої	Вашій	Вашу		Вашою	Вашій
Neuter Singular	Моє	Мого	Моєму	Мого		Моїм	Мого
	Твоє	Твого	Твоєму	Твого		Твоїм	Твого
	Наше	Нашого	Нашому	Нашого		Нашим	Нашого
	Ваше	Вашого	Вашому	Вашого		Вашим	Вашого
Plural	Мої	Моїх	Моїм	Моїх	Мої	Моїми	Моїх
	Твої	Твоїх	Твоїм	Твоїх	Твої	Твоїми	Твоїх
	Наші	Наших	Нашим	Наших	Наші	Нашими	Наших
	Ваші	Ваших	Вашим	Ваших	Ваші	Вашими	Ваших

Note that possessive pronouns 'його' (masculine), 'її' (feminine), and 'їх' (all genders) are the same for all numbers and cases, so they are not included in the table.

b. Nouns

Categories of nouns:

- Gender
- Number
- Case

Gender of nouns

There are three genders in Ukrainian: **masculine, feminine, and neuter (neutral)**. Very often grammatical gender is attributed to the noun according to physical gender, like in 'мати'– 'mother', which is feminine.

With other nouns, especially inanimate ones, it's different: the gender should be defined by the ending of the noun in its initial form, apart from a few exceptions.

Masculine			
The last letter of the word is a **hard consonant** or 'й'.	The last letter is 'ь'.	The last letter is 'а' or 'я'.	The last letter is 'о'.
For example: Журналіст – *Journalist* Край – *Region*	For example: Вчитель – *Teacher* Квітень – *April*	For example: Собака – *Dog* Суддя – *Judge*	For example: Батько – *Father* Дядько – *Uncle*

Exceptions: male names (Микола, Микита).

Feminine		
The last letter is 'а' or 'я'.	The last letter of the word is a **hard consonant**.	The last letter is 'ь'.
For example: Дочка – *Daughter* Кімната – *Room*	For example: Любов – *Love* Подорож – *Trip*	For example: Відповідь – *Answer*

Exceptions: abstract nouns (ending -ість).

Радість – *joy*, ніжність – *tenderness*, гідність – *dignity*.

Neuter		
The last letter is 'о' or 'е'.	The last letter is 'я'.	Names of young creatures (especially animals)
For example: Вікно – *Window* Море – *Sea*	**For example:** Знання – *Knowledge* Життя – *Life* Ім'я – *Name*	**For example:** Курча – *Chick* Цуценя – *Puppy*

Number of nouns

Noun type	Singular form		Plural form	
	Ending	**Example**	**Ending**	**Example**
Masculine	Hard cons.	Друг – *Friend*	-'и'	Собаки – *Dogs*
	-'й'	Музей – *Museum*	-'і'	Друзі – *Friends*
	-'ь'	Олівець – *Pencil*	-'ї'	Музеї – *Museums*
	-'а'	Собака – *Dog*		
	-'о'	Батько – *Father*		
	-'я'	Суддя – *Judge*		
Feminine	**Ending**	**Example**	**Ending**	**Example**
	Hard cons.	Любов – *Love*	-'и'	Кімнати – *Rooms*
	-'а'	Кімната – *Room*	-'і'	Відповіді – *Answers*
	-'я'	Бабуся – *Granny*		
	-'ь'	Відповідь – *Answer*		
Neuter	**Ending**	**Example**	**Ending**	**Example**
	-'о'	Вікно – *Window*	-'а'	Вікна – *Windows*
	-'е'	Море – *Sea*	-'я'	Моря – *Seas*
	-'я'	Ім'я – *Name*		
	-'а'	Курча – *Chick*		

Note: in Ukrainian, some nouns have only one form, either singular or plural.

Cases of nouns – singular

Case	Endings		
	Masculine	**Feminine**	**Neuter**
Nominative	-й, -а, -о, soft cons., hard cons.	-а, -я, -и, soft cons., hard cons.	-о, -е, -я, -а
Genitive	-а, -и, -у, -ю, -я	-и, -і, -ї	-а, -я, -и, -і
Dative	-і, -у, -ю, -ові, -еві, -єві	-і, -ї	-і, -у, -ю,- ові
Accusative	-а, -я, -у	-у, -ю, -ь	-а, -я, -е, -о
Instrumental	-ою, - ом, -ем, -єм	-ю, -ою, -ею, -єю	-ам, -ям, -ем, -ом
Locative	-і, -ї, -у, -ю, -еві, - єві, -ові	-і, -ї	-і

Cases of nouns – plural

Case	Endings		
	Masculine	**Feminine**	**Neuter**
Nominative	-и, -і, -ї	-и, -і, -ї	-а, -я, -і
Genitive	-ів, -їв	-ь, -ей, -ій, -ів, -й	-ей, -ів, -ь
Dative	-ам, -ям	-ам, -ям	-ам, -ям
Accusative	-ї, -и, -ів	-і, -ї, -и, -й	-а, -я, -і
Instrumental	-ами, - ями	-ами, -ями	-ами, -ями, -има
Locative	-ах, -ях	-ах, -ях	-ах, -ях

Note: in Ukrainian, certain neuter nouns don't depend on cases and are always the same (кіно – *cinema*, таксі – *taxi*).

c. Adjectives

Adjectives coincide with the nouns they define in gender, number, and case.

Masculine – Singular		
	hard ending (-ий)	**soft ending (-ій)**
Nominative	Червоний – *red*	Стародавній – *ancient*
Genitive	Червоного	Стародавнього
Dative	Червоному	Стародавньому
Accusative	Червоного	Стародавнього
Instrumental	Червоним	Стародавнім
Locative	Червоному	Стародавньому

Feminine – Singular		
	hard ending (-a)	**soft ending (-я)**
Nominative	Червона	Стародавня
Genitive	Червоної	Стародавньої
Dative	Червоній	Стародавній
Accusative	Червону	Стародавню
Instrumental	Червоною	Стародавньою
Locative	Червоній	Стародавній

Neuter – Singular		
	hard ending (-e)	soft ending (-є)
Nominative	Червоне	Стародавнє
Genitive	Червоного	Стародавнього
Dative	Червоному	Стародавньому
Accusative	Червоного	Стародавнього
Instrumental	Червоним	Стародавнім
Locative	Червоному	Стародавньому

Plural – All genders		
	hard ending (-i)	soft ending (-'i)
Nominative	Червоні	Стародавні
Genitive	Червоних	Стародавніх
Dative	Червоним	Стародавнім
Accusative	Червоних	Стародавніх
Instrumental	Червоними	Стародавніми
Locative	Червоних	Стародавніх

d. Verbs

Categories of verbs (included minimum)

- Person (1st, 2nd, 3rd)
- Tense

Present Tense

The Ukrainian present tense corresponds to the English present simple and present continuous.

Pronoun/Person	Ending	Example
я (1st person singular)	-у, -ю, -я	Я йду. – *I go.* Я плаваю. – *I swim.* Я вчуся. – *I study.*
ти (2nd person singular)	-еш, -єш	Ти їдеш. – *You drive.* Ти плаваєш. – *You swim.*
він, вона (3rd person singular)	-е, -є, -ить	Вона грає. – *She plays.* Він говорить. – *He speaks.*
ми (1st person plural)	-емо, -ємо, -имо	Ми граємо. – *We play.* Ми говоримо. – *We speak.*
ви (2nd person plural)	-ете, -єте, -ите	Ви граєте. – *You play.* Ви говорите. – *You speak.*
вони (3rd person plural)	-уть, -ють, - ать, -ять	Вони грають. – *They play.* Вони говорять. – *They speak.*

Past Tense

The Ukrainian past tense corresponds to the English past simple, past continuous, present perfect, past perfect, and past perfect continuous.

The ending depends on the gender of subject, i.e., the doer of the action.

Masculine	-в
Купити – *buy*	
Тато (він) купив продукти на базарі. – Dad (he) bought foodstuffs at the market.	
Feminine	**-ла**
Приїхати – *come by vehicle*	
Моя сестра (вона) приїхала сюди на автобусі. – My sister (she) came here by bus.	
Neuter	**-ло**
Сяяти – *shine*	
Вчора сяяло сонце (воно). – The sun (it) was shining yesterday.	
Plural	**-и, -ли**
Фотографувати – *take photos*	
Туристи фотографували площу. – The tourists were taking photos of the square.	

Future Tense

The Ukrainian future tense corresponds to the English future simple, future simple continuous, future perfect, and future perfect continuous.

Person	Compound form *бути + infinitive*	Simple form *infinitive conjugated according to the rules of the present tense*
я – I	буду грати – *will play*	пограю – *will play*
ти – you	будеш грати	пограєш
ми – we	будемо грати	пограємо
ви – you	будете грати	пограєте
він/вона/оно – he/she/it	буде грати	пограє
вони – they	будуть грати	пограють

e. Numerals

1. Cardinal numerals

Please note the frequent use of the soft sign ('ь')

0	Нуль	20	Двадцять
1	Один	30	Тридцять
2	Два	40	Сорок
3	Три	50	П'ятдесят
4	Чотири	60	Шістдесят
5	П'ять	70	Сімдесят
6	Шість	80	Вісімдесят
7	Сім	90	Дев'яносто
8	Вісім	100	Сто

9	Дев'ять	200	Двісті
10	Десять	300	Триста
11	Одинадцять	400	Чотириста
12	Дванадцять	500	П'ятсот
13	Тринадцять	600	Шістсот
14	Чотирнадцять	700	Сімсот
15	П'ятнадцять	800	Вісімсот
16	Шістнадцять	900	Дев'ятсот
17	Сімнадцять	1000	Тисяча
18	Вісімнадцять		
19	Дев'ятнадцять		

2. Ordinal numerals

	Masculine (ending -ий, -ій)	Feminine (ending -а, -я)	Neuter (ending -е, -є)
1st	Перший	Перша	Перше
2nd	Другий	Друга	Друге
3rd	Третій	Третя	Третє
4th	Четвертий	Четверта	Четверте
5th	П'ятий	П'ята	П'яте
6th	Шостий	Шоста	Шосте
7th	Сьомий	Сьома	Сьоме
8th	Восьмий	Восьма	Восьме
9th	Дев'ятий	Дев'ята	Дев'яте
10th	Десятий	Десята	Десяте
11th	Одинадцятий	Одинадцята	Одинадцяте
12th	Дванадцятий	Дванадцята	Дванадцяте
13th	Тринадцятий	Тринадцята	Тринадцяте
14th	Чотирнадцятий	Чотирнадцята	Чотирнадцяте
15th	П'ятнадцятий	П'ятнадцята	П'ятнадцяте
16th	Шістнадцятий	Шістнадцята	Шістнадцяте
17th	Сімнадцятий	Сімнадцята	Сімнадцяте
18th	Вісімнадцятий	Вісімнадцята	Вісімнадцяте
19th	Дев'ятнадцятий	Дев'ятнадцята	Дев'ятнадцяте
20th	Двадцятий	Двадцята	Двадцяте
30th	Тридцятий	Тридцята	Тридцяте
40th	Сороковий	Сорокова	Сорокове
50th	П'ятдесятий	П'ятдесята	П'ятдесяте
60th	Шістдесятий	Шістдесята	Шістдесяте

70th	Сімдесятий	Сімдесята	Сімдесяте
80th	Вісімдесятий	Вісімдесята	Вісімдесяте
90th	Дев'яностий	Дев'яноста	Дев'яносте
100th	Сотий	Сота	Соте
200th	Двохсотий	Двохсота	Двохсоте
300th	Трьохсотий	Трьохсота	Трьохсоте
400th	Чотирьохсотий	Чотирьохсота	Чотирьохсоте
500th	П'ятисотий	П'ятисота	П'ятисоте
600th	Шістсотий	Шістсота	Шістсоте
700th	Сімсотий	Сімсота	Сімсоте
800th	Вісімсотий	Вісімсота	Вісімсоте
900th	Дев'ятсотий	Дев'ятсота	Дев'ятсоте
1000th	Тисячний	Тисячна	Тисячне

III.   A few peculiarities that are essential for better understanding

The verb 'бути' – 'to be'

Compare these sentences in Ukrainian and English:

Я пілот – I am a pilot

These sentences mean the same thing but have a different number of words. The thing is that the Ukrainian verb 'to be' – 'бути' is omitted in the present tense. **Compare more examples:**

Він з Европи. – He is from Europe.

Вони спокійні та доброзичливі. – They are calm and friendly.

Вони мої батьки. – They are my parents.

Я письменник та художник. – I am a writer and an artist.

Types of sentences and their word order

Affirmative sentences

In the English language, affirmative sentences always follow the Subject (S) + Verb (V) + Object (O) pattern, while this structure can be rather flexible in Ukrainian. The S+V+O pattern is the most widespread one, but you can also come across O+V+S or V+S+O options.

The difference between them is in the shades of meaning.

Example:

Ми грали в бадмінтон. – We were playing badminton. – Neutral meaning.

22

В бадмінтон грали ми. – The same translation with the emphasis on the game we were playing. That it was badminton and not tennis or basketball.

Грали ми в бадмінтон. – The emphasis is on the action.

Conclusion: While you can play with the word order in affirmative sentences, every time you don't feel confident, go for the typical S+V+O structure, and you'll make no mistake. Over time and with more practice, you'll learn to "feel" the word order.

Negative sentences

There are four particles in Ukrainian that help express negation - **'ні', 'не', 'нема' / 'немає'** **(these two are often interchangeable).**

Take a look at these examples to get a general idea without going into much detail.

Ти рано прокидаєшся на вихідних? – *Ні, на вихідних я прокидаюся пізно.*

Do you wake up early on weekends? – *No, I don't. I wake up late on weekends*.*

У кімнаті **нема / немає** лікаря. – *There is no doctor in the room.*

У мене **нема / немає кота.** – *I don't have a cat.*

Я **не** граю на гітарі. – *I don't play the guitar.*

Це **не** мій будинок. – *This is not my house.*

У неї немає **ні** дітей, **ні** чоловіка. – *She's got neither kids nor a husband.*

*In Ukrainian, there is negation and affirmation in one sentence, and this is absolutely normal. First you negate the question about waking up early and then say that you wake up late in the same sentence.

Interrogative sentences

Finally, unlike in English, interrogative sentences in Ukrainian don't require any grammatical change of the sentence. If it's **a question with the question word**, we just add it to the initial affirmative sentence, make the corresponding changes in pronouns, and change the intonation.

For example:

Мене звати Таня (in daily life, you can also use the shortened answer: Таня).
The question version of this sentence is: **Як тебе звати?**

Мені десять років (in daily life, you can also use the shortened answer: Десять).
The question version of this sentence is: **Скільки тобі років?**

If it's **a yes/no question**, we simply change the pronoun and the intonation.

For example:

У мене є сім'я.
The question version of this sentence is: **У тебе є сім'я?**

Я розмовляю італійською.
The question version of this sentence is: **Ти розмовляєш італійською?**

Finally, let's learn 12 interesting facts about the Ukrainian language:

1. The Ukrainian language is one of the most melodic languages in the world. In 1934, at a linguistic congress in Paris, renowned experts agreed that Ukrainian was the third most beautiful language (after French and Persian) based on phonetics, vocabulary, phraseology, and sentence structure. Years later, at a forum of linguists in Switzerland, the Ukrainian language took the honorary second place as the most melodic language after Italian.

2. About 41–45 million people speak the Ukrainian language. In terms of vocabulary, the languages closest to Ukrainian are Belarusian, Polish, Serbian, and only after that—Russian. As for phonetics and grammar, Ukrainian is most similar to Belarusian, Czech, Slovak, and Polish.

3. Linguist and researcher Vasyl Kobyliukh proved that the Ukrainian language was formed in the X–IV centuries BCE and that it derived from Sanskrit.

4. The modern Ukrainian language has about 256 thousand words.

5. Ukrainian was the official language of the Kuban People's Republic in 1918-1920.

6. The Ukrainian language is exceptionally rich in diminutive forms and synonyms, making it very versatile and cute.

7. In Ukrainian, there are three forms of the future tense (simple, compound, and complex).

8. The Ukrainian language is semi-official in Cook County (Illinois, USA). This area (including Chicago) has a large Ukrainian community. Consequently, Ukrainian is one of the most widely spoken languages in the county.

9. During the 18th and 19th centuries, Ukrainians used about 50 different writing systems. In terms of complexity, Ukrainian orthography/spelling is ahead even of Mongolian—one of the most difficult languages in the world.

10. About 40% of the Ukrainian language queries on Yandex (the top Russian search engine and web portal) are related to science and education.

11. The first Ukrainian ABC book ("Абетка") was published in Lviv in 1574 by Ivan Fyodorov, the pioneer of printing. Only one copy of the book, found in Rome in 1927, has survived. Nowadays, this ancient edition is available in the library of Harvard University.

12. The Ukrainian language has many different dialects. Often, people from the eastern region of Ukraine don't understand people from the west.

Now, let's get started with the content!

ЕМОЦІЇ (EMOTIONS)

1) **щасливий** (happy)
schas-LY-vyj

2) **сумний** (sad)
sum-NYJ

3) **радий** (excited)
RA-dyj

4) **злий** (angry)
zlyj

5) **здивований** (surprised)
zdy-VO-va-nyj

6) **стурбований** (concerned)
stur-BO-va-nyj

7) **наляканий** (scared)
na-L'A-ka-nyj

8) **допитливий** (curious)
do-pyt-LY-vyj

9) **веселий** (amused)
ve-SE-lyj

10) **збентежений** (confused)
zben-TE-zhe-nyj

11) **хворий** (sick)
KHVO-ryj

12) **неслухняний** (naughty)
ne-sluh-N'A-nyj

13) **серйозний** (serious)
ser'-YOZ-nyj

14) **зосереджений** (focused)
zo-se-RE-dzhe-nyj

15) **знуджений** (bored)
ZNUD-zhe- nyj

16) **приголомшений** (overwhelmed)
pry-ho-LOM-she-nyj

17) **закоханий** (in love)
za-KO-ha-nyj

18) **присоромлений** (ashamed)
pry-so-ROM-le-nyj

19) **занепокоєний** (anxious)
za-ne-po-KO-ye-nyj

20) **той, що відчуває огиду** (disgusted)
toj, shho vidchuVAye oHYdu

21) **ображений** (offended)
ob-RA-zhe-nyj

22) **болісний** (sore)
BO-lis-nyj

Чому ти сьогодні такий серйозний?
Why are you so serious today?

Він завжди зосереджений на роботі.
He is always focused at work.

Мої колеги збентежені цим проєктом.
My colleagues are confused with this project.

СІМ'Я (THE FAMILY)

1) **дідусь і бабуся** (grandparents)
   di-DUS' i ba-BU-s'a

2) **бабуся** (grandmother)
   ba-BU-s'a

3) **дідусь** (grandfather)
   di-DUS'

4) **дядько** (uncle)
   D'AD'-ko

5) **мати** (mother)
   MA-ty

6) **батько** (father)
   BAT'-ko

7) **тітка** (aunt)
   TIT-ka

8) **двоюрідний брат** (cousin, m.)
   dvo-YU-rid-nyj brat

9) **брат** (brother)
   brat

10) **дружина** (wife)
    dru-ZHY-na

11) **чоловік** (husband)
    cho-lo-VIK

12) **сестра** (sister)
    ses-TRA

13) **двоюрідна сестра** (cousin, f.)
    dvo-YU-rid-na ses-TRA

14) **племінник** (nephew)
    ple-MIN-nyk

15) **син** (son)
    syn

16) **дочка** (daughter)
    doch-KA

17) **племінниця** (niece)
    ple-MIN-ny-ts'a

18) **внук** (grandson)
    vnuk

19) **внучка** (granddaughter)
    VNU-chka

20) **троюрідний брат** (second cousin, m.)
    tro-YU-rid-nyj brat

- **Сім'я чоловіка/дружини (In-laws)
  – Родичі (Relatives)**

  Si-M'YA cho-lo-VI-ka/dru-ZHY-ny

  – RO-dy-chi

21) **свекор/тесть** (father-in-law)
    SVE-kor/test'

22) **свекруха/теща** (mother-in-law)
    svek-RU-ha/TE-scha

23) **свояк/шурин** (brother-in-law)
    svo-YAK/SHU-ryn

24) **своячка/зовиця** (sister-in-law)
    svo-YACH-ka/zo-VY-ts'a

25) **невістка** (daughter-in-law)
    ne-VIST-ka

26) **зять** (son-in-law)
    z'at'

27) **дядько чоловіка/дружини** (uncle-in-law)
    D'AD'-ko cho-lo-VI-ka/dru-ZHY-ny

28) **тітка чоловіка/дружини** (aunt-in-law)
    TIT-ka cho-lo-VI-ka/dru-ZHY-ny

Моя племінниця вже ходить до школи.
My niece already goes to school.

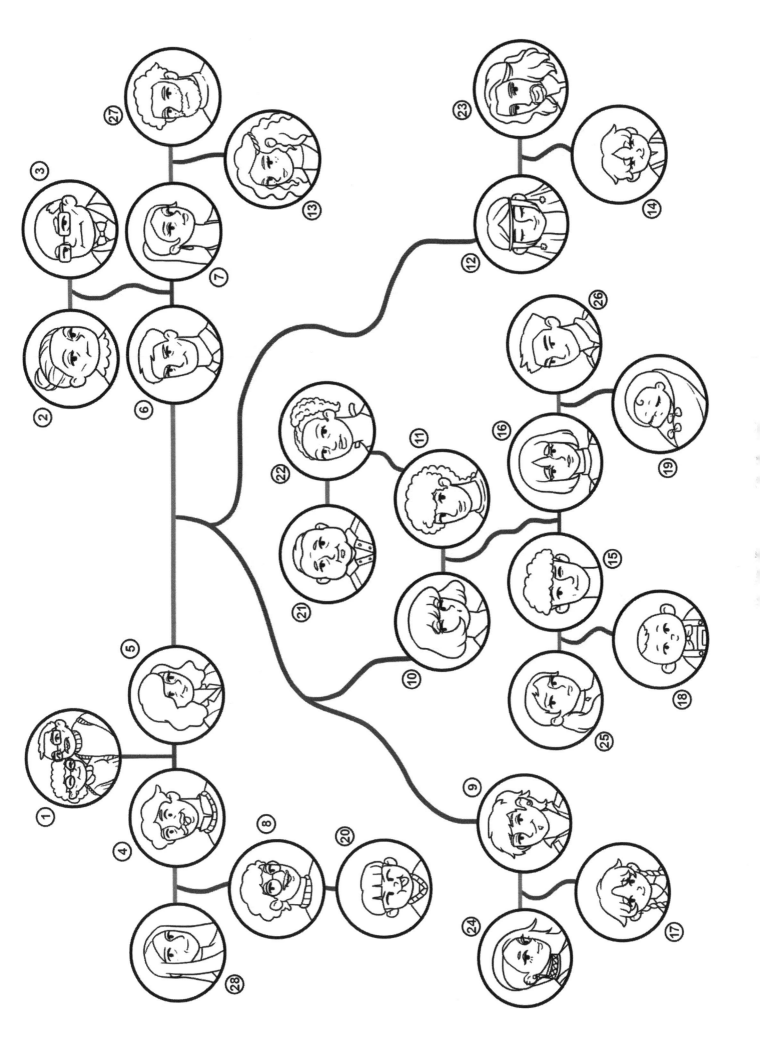

СТОСУНКИ (RELATIONSHIPS)

1) **подружня пара** (married couple)
pod-RUZH-n'a PA-ra

2) **одружений чоловік** (married man)
od-RU-zhe-nyj cho-lo-VIK

3) **заміжня жінка** (married woman)
za-MIZH-n'a ZHIN-ka

4) **розлучена пара** (divorced couple)
roz-LU-che-na PA-ra

5) **колишня дружина** (ex-wife)
ko-LYSH-n'a dru-ZHY-na

6) **колишній чоловік** (ex-husband)
ko-LYSH-nij cho-lo-VIK

7) **друг** (friend)
druh

8) **дівчина** (girlfriend)
DIV-chy-na

9) **хлопець** (boyfriend)
KHLO-pets'

10) **сусід** (neighbor)
su-SID

11) **неодружений/незаміжня** (single, m/f)
ne-od-RU-zhe-nyj/ne-za-MIZH-n'a

12) **розлучений/розлучена, розлучення** (divorced m/f, divorce)
roz-LU-che-nyj/roz-LU-che-na, roz-LU-chen-n'a

13) **вдівець** (widower)
vdi-VETS'

14) **вдова** (widow)
vdo-VA

Максим – мій найкращий друг.
Maksym is my best friend.

Моя колишня дружина живе в іншому місті.
My ex-wife lives in another town.

Ця подружня пара – наші сусіди.
The married couple are our neighbors.

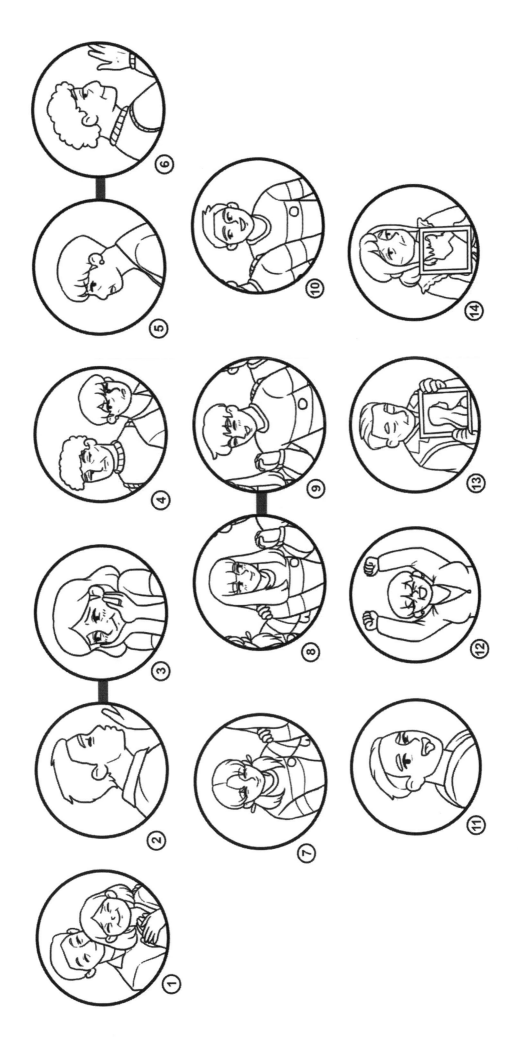

ЦІННОСТІ (VALUES)

1) **повага** (respect)
   po-VA-ha

2) **вдячність** (gratitude)
   VD'ACH-nist'

3) **толерантність** (tolerance)
   to-le-RANT-nist'

4) **взаємодопомога** (mutual aid)
   vza-ye-mo-do-po-MO-ha

5) **чесність** (honesty)
   CHES-nist'

6) **стриманість, помірність**
   (temperance)
   STRY-ma-nist', po-MIR-nist'

7) **відповідальність** (responsibility)
   vid-po-vi-DAL'-nist'

8) **віра** (faith)
   VI-ra

9) **мужність** (courage)
   MUZH-nist'

10) **доброта** (kindness)
    do-bro-TA

11) **зобов'язання** (commitment)
    zo-bo-v'ya-ZAN-n'a

12) **ентузіазм** (enthusiasm)
    en-tu-zi-AZM

13) **довіра** (trust)
    do-VI-ra

14) **пунктуальність** (punctuality)
    punk-tu-AL'-nist'

Я дуже ціную твою чесність.
I appreciate your honesty a lot.

У нього величезне терпіння.
He has great patience.

Вона назавжди втратила мою довіру.
She's lost my trust forever.

ТІЛО ЛЮДИНИ (THE HUMAN BODY)

1) **голова** (head)
ho-lo-VA

2) **волосся** (hair)
vo-LOS'-s'a

3) **обличчя** (face)
ob-LYCH-ch'a

4) **чоло** (forehead)
cho-LO

5) **вухо** (ear)
VU-ho

6) **очі** (eyes)
O-chi

7) **ніс** (nose)
nis

8) **щока** (cheek)
scho-KA

9) **рот** (mouth)
rot

10) **підборіддя** (chin)
pid-bo-RID-d'a

11) **шия** (neck)
SHY-ya

12) **спина** (back)
SPY-na

13) **груди** (chest)
HRU-dy

14) **плече** (shoulder)
ple-CHE

15) **рука** (arm)
ru-KA

16) **передпліччя** (forearm)
pe-red-PLICH-cha

17) **долоня** (hand)
do-LO-n'a

18) **живіт** (abdomen)
zhy-VIT

19) **талія** (waist)
TA-li-ya

20) **сідниці** (buttocks)
sid-NY-tsi

21) **нога** (leg)
no-HA

22) **стегно** (thigh)
steh-NO

23) **коліно** (knee)
ko-LI-no

24) **литка** (calf)
LYT-ka

25) **гомілка** (shin)
ho-MIL-ka

26) **стопа** (foot)
sto-PA

У неї гарні зелені очі.
She's got beautiful green eyes.

Вона впала і зламала руку.
She fell down and broke her arm.

Я роблю вправи, щоб спина не боліла.
I do exercises so that my back doesn't hurt.

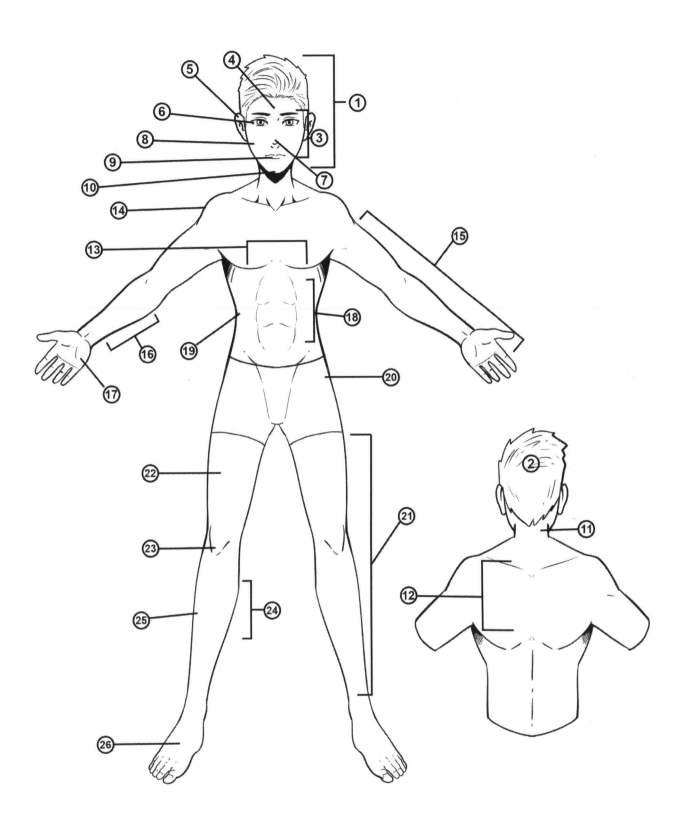

ВНУТРІШНІ ОРГАНИ ЛЮДИНИ (INSIDE THE HUMAN BODY)

1) **шкіра** (skin)
SHKI-ra

2) **м'язи** (muscles)
M'YA-zy

3) **кістки** (bones)
kist-KY

4) **мозок** (brain)
MO-zok

5) **щитовидна залоза** (thyroid)
schy-to-VYD-na ZA-lo-za

6) **вени** (veins)
VE-ny

7) **артерії** (arteries)
ar-TE-ri-yi

8) **серце** (heart)
SER-tse

9) **легені** (lungs)
le-HE-ni

10) **шлунок** (stomach)
SHLU-nok

11) **стравохід** (esophagus)
stra-vo-KHID

12) **підшлункова залоза** (pancreas)
pid-shlun-KO-va ZA-lo-za

13) **печінка** (liver)
pe-CHIN-ka

14) **тонка кишка** (small intestine)
ton-KA KYSH-ka

15) **товста кишка** (large intestine)
tovs-TA KYSH-ka

16) **жовчний міхур** (gallbladder)
ZHOVCH-nyj mi-KHUR

17) **нирки** (kidneys)
NYR-ky

18) **сечовий міхур** (urinary bladder)
se-cho-VYJ mi-KHUR

У моєї бабусі проблеми з серцем.
My grandmother has heart issues.

Смажена їжа шкідлива для шлунка.
Fried food is bad for the stomach.

Йому видалили жовчний міхур.
He had his gallbladder removed.

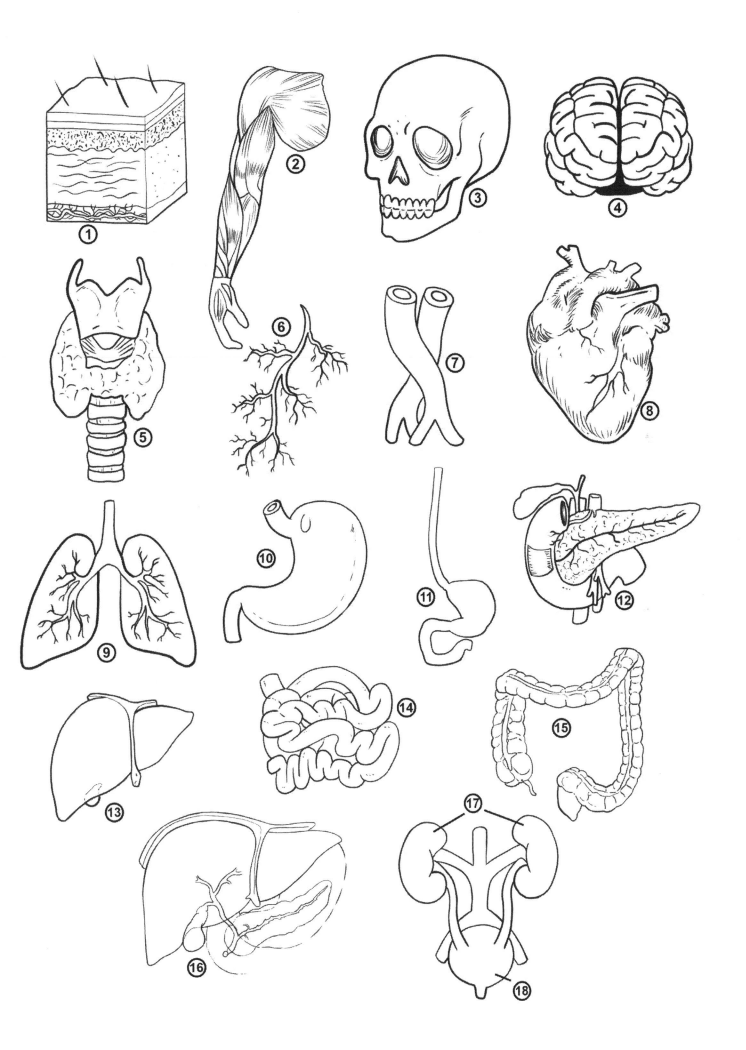

ДОМАШНІ ТВАРИНИ (PETS)

1) **собака** (dog)
   so-BA-ka

2) **кіт/кішка** (cat m./f.)
   kit/KISH-ka

3) **тхір** (ferret)
   tkhir

4) **міні-піг** (mini pig/teacup pig)
   mi-ni-PIH

5) **кінь** (horse)
   kin'

6) **скалярія** (angelfish)
   ska-L'A-ri-ya

7) **риба-клоун** (clown fish)
   RY-ba KLO-un

8) **золота рибка** (goldfish)
   zo-lo-TA RYB-ka

9) **хом'як** (hamster)
   kho-M'YAK

10) **морська свинка** (guinea pig)
    mors'-KA SVYN-ka

11) **миша** (mouse)
    MY-sha

12) **кролик** (rabbit)
    KRO-lyk

13) **їжак** (hedgehog)
    yi-ZHAK

14) **тарантул** (tarantula)
    ta-RAN-tul

15) **колонія мурах** (ant colony)
    ko-LO-ni-ya mu-RAKH

16) **черепаха** (tortoise)
    che-re-PA-kha

17) **змія** (snake)
    zmi-YA

18) **хамелеон** (chameleon)
    kha-me-le-ON

19) **ігуана** (iguana)
    i-gu-A-na

20) **канарка** (canary)
    ka-NAR-ka

21) **папуга** (parrot)
    pa-PU-ha

22) **довгохвостий папуга** (parakeet)
    dov-ho-KHVOS-tyj pa-PU-ha

У мене дві собаки і один кіт.
I've got two dogs and one cat.

Мама боїться мого тарантула.
My mom is afraid of my tarantula.

Дядько купив моїй сестрі золоту рибку.
My uncle has bought my sister a goldfish.

ЗООПАРК (THE ZOO)

1) **слон** (elephant)
slon

2) **носоріг** (rhinoceros)
no-so-RIH

3) **жираф** (giraffe)
zhy-RAF

4) **зебра** (zebra)
ZE-bra

5) **бегемот** (hippopotamus)
be-he-MOT

6) **гепард** (cheetah)
he-PARD

7) **тигр** (tiger)
tyhr

8) **лев** (lion)
lev

9) **шимпанзе** (chimpanzee)
shym-pan-ZE

10) **орангутанг** (orangutan)
o-ran-hu-TANH

11) **бабуїн** (baboon)
ba-bu-YIN

12) **кенгуру** (kangaroo)
ken-hu-RU

13) **коала** (koala)
ko-A-la

14) **лемур** (lemur)
le-MUR

Жираф – найвища тварина у світі.
The giraffe is the tallest animal on Earth.

Тигр сильніший за лева.
The tiger is stronger than the lion.

Зебри схожі на коней.
Zebras resemble horses.

ПТАХИ (BIRDS)

1) **страус** (ostrich)
STRA-us

2) **павич** (peacock)
pa-VYCH

3) **індичка** (turkey)
in-DYCH-ka

4) **півень** (rooster)
PI-ven'

5) **качка** (duck)
KACH-ka

6) **лебідь** (swan)
LE-bid'

7) **пелікан** (pelican)
pe-li-KAN

8) **фламінго** (flamingo)
fla-MIN-ho

9) **голуб** (pigeon)
HO-lub

10) **сова** (owl)
so-VA

11) **стерв'ятник** (vulture)
ster-V'YAT-nyk

12) **орел** (eagle)
o-REL

13) **чайка** (seagull)
CHAJ-ka

14) **ворона** (crow)
vo-RO-na

15) **тукан** (toucan)
tu-KAN

16) **пінгвін** (penguin)
pinh-VIN

17) **дятел** (woodpecker)
D'A-tel

18) **ара** (macaw)
A-ra

19) **колібрі** (hummingbird)
ko-LIB-ri

20) **ківі** (kiwi)
KI-vi

Орел – це сильний, хижий птах.
The eagle is a strong, carnivorous bird.

Мені не потрібен будильник, тому що у мене є півень
I don't need an alarm clock because I've got a rooster.

Качки полюбляють плавати і пірнати.
Ducks love swimming and diving.

QUIZ #1

Use arrows to match English words with their corresponding Ukrainian translations:

a. husband

b. eagle

c. naughty

d. dog

e. hair

f. elephant

g. aunt

h. brain

i. tiger

j. daughter

k. faith

l. girlfriend

m. skin

n. curious

o. respect

p. swan

1. собака

2. слон

3. мозок

4. шкіра

5. віра

6. повага

7. тигр

8. чоловік

9. допитливий

10. орел

11. тітка

12. лебідь

13. дочка

14. волосся

15. дівчина

16. неслухняний

Fill in the blank spaces with the options below (use each word only once):

Маленький Матвій сьогодні _____. Він плаче; його обличчя та _____ червоні від сліз. Бабуся обіцяла відвести його до зоопарку. Матвій обожнює тварин. У нього є кролик, ігуана та _____. Але вони не можуть поїхати до зоопарку, бо автомобіль зламався. «Матвію, не плач, – просить бабуся, – ти краєш мені _____. Ти мій улюблений _____, але я не можу полагодити автомобіль сама!». Матвій розуміє, але не може заспокоїтись. Віктор Іванович – _____ бабусі. Він пропонує відвезти їх до зоопарку своїм автомобілем. Тепер Матвій _____. Він побачив бегемота, жирафа, гепарда і навіть _____! Із птахів йому дуже сподобалися ара та _____.

«Дякую, – каже бабуся, – ваша _____ врятувала мого внука!

–Нема за що, – відповідає Віктор Іванович, – щаслива дитина – це найкраща _____».

сусід	очі
сумний	лева
хом'як	внук
подяка	щасливий
серце	доброта
бабуся	ківі

РЕПТИЛІЇ І АМФІБІЇ (REPTILES AND AMPHIBIANS)

- **Рептилії (Reptiles)**
  rep-TY-li-yi

1) **анаконда** (anaconda)
   a-na-KON-da

2) **королівська кобра** (king cobra)
   ko-ro-LIVS'-ka KOB-ra

3) **гримуча змія** (rattlesnake)
   hry-MU-cha zmi-YA

4) **коралова змія** (coral snake)
   ko-RA-lo-va zmi-YA

5) **рогата ящірка** (horned lizard)
   ro-HA-ta YA-schir-ka

6) **плащоносна ящірка** (frill-necked lizard)
   pla-scho-NOS-na YA-schir-ka

7) **звичайний василіск/ящірка**
   (common basilisk/Jesus Christ lizard)
   zvy-CHAJ-nyj va-sy-LISK

8) **комодський варан** (Komodo dragon)
   ko-MODS'-kyj va-RAN

9) **крокодил** (crocodile)
   kro-ko-DYL

10) **гавіал** (gharial/gavial)
    ha-vi-AL

11) **морська черепаха** (sea turtle)
    mors'-KA che-re-PA-ha

- **Амфібії (Amphibians)**
  am-FI-bi-yi

12) **саламандра** (salamander)
    sa-la-MAN-dra

13) **жаба-голіаф** (Goliath frog)
    ZHA-ba ho-li-AF

Крокодили жили одночасно з динозаврами.
Crocodiles lived at the same time as dinosaurs.

Королівська кобра гарна, але дуже небезпечна.
The royal cobra looks beautiful, but it's very dangerous.

Анаконда не отруйна, але дуже сильна змія.
The anaconda is not a poisonous snake, but a very strong one.

КОМАХИ І ПАВУКОПОДІБНІ (INSECTS AND ARACHNIDS)

- **Комахи (Insects)**
  ko-MA-khy

1) **бджола** (bee)
   bdzho-LA

2) **джміль** (bumblebee)
   dzhmil'

3) **оса** (wasp)
   o-SA

4) **жук** (beetle)
   zhuk

5) **метелик** (butterfly)
   me-TE-lyk

6) **міль** (moth)
   mil'

7) **бабка** (dragonfly)
   BAB-ka

8) **сонечко** (ladybug)
   SO-nech-ko

9) **світлячок** (firefly)
   svit-l'a-CHOK

10) **тарган** (cockroach)
    tar-HAN

11) **ґедзь** (horsefly)
    gedz'

12) **муха** (fly)
    MU-kha

13) **комар** (mosquito)
    ko-MAR

14) **коник** (grasshopper)
    KO-nyk

15) **цвіркун** (cricket)
    tsvir-KUN

- **Павукоподібні (Arachnids)**
  pa-vu-ko-po-DIB-ni

16) **скорпіон** (scorpion)
    skor-pi-ON

17) **павук** (spider)
    pa-VUK

18) **чорна вдова** (southern black widow)
    CHOR-na vdo-VA

Багато людей бояться павуків.
Many people are afraid of spiders.

Бабки схожі на маленькі вертольоти.
Dragonflies resemble little helicopters.

Мою дочку вжалила оса.
My daughter was stung by a wasp.

ССАВЦІ I (MAMMALS I)

1) **кажан** (bat)
ka-ZHAN

2) **качкодзьоб** (platypus)
kach-ko-DZ'OB

3) **косатка** (killer whale/orca)
ko-SAT-ka

4) **дельфін** (dolphin)
del'-FIN

5) **бобер** (beaver)
bo-BER

6) **бабак** (groundhog)
ba-BAK

7) **кріт** (mole)
krit

8) **білка** (squirrel)
BIL-ka

9) **ласка** (weasel)
LAS-ka

10) **опосум** (opossum)
o-PO-sum

11) **щур** (rat)
schur

12) **заєць** (hare)
ZA-yets'

13) **борсук** (badger)
bor-SUK

14) **скунс** (skunk)
skuns

15) **леопард** (leopard)
le-o-PARD

Опосуми носять своїх малюків на спині.
Possums carry their babies on their backs.

Чи правда, що скунси жахливо пахнуть?
Is it true that skunks smell awful?

Кажуть, що дельфіни дуже розумні.
Dolphins are said to be very intelligent.

ССАВЦІ II (MAMMALS II)

1) **ведмідь** (bear)
ved-MID'

2) **гієна** (hyena)
hi-YE-na

3) **шакал** (jackal)
sha-KAL

4) **корова** (cow)
ko-RO-va

5) **бик** (bull)
byk

6) **лисиця** (fox)
ly-SY-ts'a

7) **бізон/буйвол** (buffalo)
bi-ZON/BUJ-vol

8) **лось** (elk/moose)
los'

9) **вівця** (sheep)
viv-TS'A

10) **коза** (goat)
ko-ZA

11) **газель** (gazelle)
ha-ZEL'

12) **вовк** (wolf)
vovk

13) **мавпа** (monkey)
MAV-pa

14) **баран** (ram)
ba-RAN

15) **осел** (donkey)
o-SEL

Ви знали, що ведмеді можуть швидко бігати?
Did you know that bears can run fast?

Вовки часто нападають на овець.
Wolves often attack sheep.

Корови і кози дають людям молоко.
Cows and goats give people milk.

РИБИ І МОЛЮСКИ (FISH AND MOLLUSKS)

- **Риби (Fish)**
  RY-by

1) **китова акула** (whale shark)
   ky-TO-va a-KU-la

2) **біла акула** (white shark)
   BI-la a-KU-la

3) **акула-молот** (hammerhead shark)
   a-KU-la MO-lot

4) **риба-меч** (swordfish/marlin)
   RY-ba mech

5) **баракуда** (barracuda)
   ba-ra-KU-da

6) **риба фугу** (pufferfish)
   RY-ba FU-hu

7) **сом** (catfish)
   som

8) **піранья** (piranha)
   pi-RAN'-YA

9) **летюча риба** (flying fish)
   le-T'U-cha RY-ba

10) **мурена** (moray eel)
    mu-RE-na

11) **скат манта** (manta ray)
    skat MAN-ta

12) **морський коник** (seahorse)
    mors'-KYJ KO-nyk

- **Молюски (Mollusks)**
  mo-L'U-sky

13) **кальмар** (squid)
    kal'-MAR

14) **каракатиця** (cuttlefish)
    ka-ra-KA-ty-ts'a

15) **восьминіг** (octopus)
    vos'-my-NIH

16) **устриця** (oyster)
    U-stry-ts'a

17) **молюск** (clam)
    mo-L'USK

18) **наутилус** (nautilus)
    na-u-TY-lus

19) **равлик** (snail)
    RAV-lyk

20) **слимак** (slug)
    sly-MAK

Морськи коники такі милі!
Seahorses are so cute!

Восьминоги можуть бути і крихітними, і величезними.
Octopuses can be both tiny and huge.

Піраній приваблює запах крові.
Piranhas are attracted by the smell of blood.

ОДЯГ I (CLOTHING I)

1) **плащ** (raincoat)
   plasch

2) **кенгуринка** (hoodie)
   ken-hu-RYN-ka

3) **куртка** (jacket)
   KURT-ka

4) **джинси** (jeans)
   DZHYN-sy

5) **труси-боксери** (boxer shorts)
   tru-SY bok-SE-ry

6) **чоботи** (boots)
   CHO-bo-ty

7) **сережки** (earrings)
   se-REZH-ky

8) **светр** (sweater)
   svetr

9) **намисто** (necklace)
   na-MYS-to

10) **бюстгальтер** (bra)
    b'ust-HAL'-ter

11) **лосини** (leggings)
    lo-SY-ny

12) **шкарпетки** (socks)
    shkar-PET-ky

13) **блузка/топ** (blouse/top)
    BLUZ-ka/top

14) **браслет** (bracelet)
    bras-LET

15) **шорти** (shorts)
    SHOR-ty

16) **трусики** (panties)
    TRU-sy-ky

17) **пальто** (coat)
    pal'-TO

18) **сукня** (dress)
    SUK-n'a

19) **сумочка** (purse)
    SU-moch-ka

20) **сандалі** (sandals)
    san-DA-li

Мені подобаються браслети та сережки.
I like bracelets and earrings.

Хтось бачив мою чорну куртку?
Has anybody seen my black jacket?

Моя племінниця не любить носити сукні.
My niece doesn't like wearing dresses.

ОДЯГ II (CLOTHING II)

1) **капелюх** (hat)
ka-pe-L'UKH

2) **смокінг** (tuxedo)
SMO-kinh

3) **краватка-метелик** (bow tie)
kra-VAT-ka me-TE-lyk

4) **взуття** (footwear)
vzut-T'A

5) **костюм** (suit)
kos-T'UM

6) **сорочка** (shirt)
so-ROCH-ka

7) **краватка** (tie)
kra-VAT-ka

8) **портфель** (briefcase/case)
port-FEL'

9) **блузка з довгими рукавами** (long-sleeved blouse)
BLUZ-ka z DOV-hy-my ru-ka-VA-my

10) **спортивний бюстгальтер** (sports bra)
spor-TYV-nyj b'ust-HAL'-ter

11) **брюки/штани** (trousers/pants)
BR'U-ky/shta-NY

12) **пасок** (belt)
PA-sok

13) **каблучка** (ring)
kab-LUCH-ka

14) **футболка** (T-shirt)
fut-BOL-ka

15) **спідниця** (skirt)
spid-NY-ts'a

16) **шарф** (scarf)
sharf

17) **годинник** (watch)
ho-DYN-nyk

18) **штани з кишенями** (cargo pants)
shta-NY z ky-SHE-n'a-my

19) **гаманець** (wallet)
ha-ma-NETS'

20) **парасоля** (umbrella)
pa-ra-SO-l'a

Цей пасок занадто довгий для моїх штанів.
This belt is too long for my trousers.

Я хочу, щоб капелюх і сумочка були однакового кольору.
I want the hat to match the purse in color.

Взуття має бути зручним.
Footwear must be comfortable.

ПОГОДА (THE WEATHER)

1) **сонячно** (sunny)
   SO-n'ach-no

2) **спекотно** (hot)
   spe-KOT-no

3) **піщана буря** (sandstorm)
   pi-SCHA-na BU-r'a

4) **хмарно** (cloudy)
   HMAR-no

5) **тепло** (warm)
   TEP-lo

6) **туманно** (foggy/misty)
   tu-MAN-no

7) **дощова погода** (rainy)
   do-scho-VA po-HO-da

8) **прохолодно** (cool)
   pro-ho-LOD-no

9) **крапля дощу** (raindrop)
   KRAP-l'a do-SCHU

10) **волого** (humid)
    vo-LO-ho

11) **буря** (storm)
    BU-r'a

12) **блискавка** (lightning)
    BLYS-kav-ka

13) **вітряно** (windy)
    VIT-r'a-no

14) **сніжно** (snowy)
    SNIZH-no

15) **холодно** (cold)
    HO-lod-no

16) **сніжинка** (snowflake)
    sni-ZHYN-ka

Кожна сніжинка має унікальну форму.
Every snowflake has a unique shape.

Сьогодні така спека!
It's so hot today!

Вчора був дуже дощовий день.
Yesterday was a very rainy day.

ПОРИ РОКУ: ВЕСНА (THE SEASONS – SPRING)

1) **сад** (garden)
sad

2) **цвітіння/квітка** (blossom)
tsvi-TIN'-n'a/KVIT-ka

3) **пікнік** (picnic)
pik-NIK

4) **парк** (park)
park

5) **велосипедна прогулянка**
(bike ride)
ve-lo-sy-PED-na pro-HU-l'an-ka

6) **лимонад** (lemonade)
ly-mo-NAD

7) **гаражний розпродаж** (garage sale)
ha-RAZH-nyj roz-PRO-dazh

8) **поїздка** (road trip)
po-YIZD-ka

9) **фарбувати каміння** (to paint rocks)
far-bu-VA-ty ka-MIN'-n'a

10) **садити квіти** (to plant flowers)
sa-DY-ty KVI-ty

11) **запускати повітряного змія** (to fly a kite)
za-pus-KA-ty po-VIT-r'a-no-ho ZMI-ya

12) **піти на шашлики** (to attend a barbecue)
pi-TY na shash-ly-KY

На вулиці було трохи вітряно, і ми запустили повітряного змія.
It was a bit windy outside, and we flew a kite.

Навесні наш парк чудовий.
Our park is wonderful in spring.

Восени у мене багато справ у дворі.
In autumn, I've got a lot to do in the backyard.

ПОРИ РОКУ: ЛІТО (THE SEASONS – SUMMER)

1) **жити в наметах** (to go camping)
ZHY-ty v na-ME-tah

2) **аквапарк** (water park)
ak-va-PARK

3) **активний відпочинок** (outdoor activities)
ak-TYV-nyj vid-po-CHY-nok

4) **басейн** (swimming pool)
ba-SEJN

5) **плавати** (to swim)
PLA-va-ty

6) **засмагати** (to get tanned)
zas-ma-HA-ty

7) **сонцезахисний крем** (sunscreen)
son-tse-za-hys-NYJ krem

8) **спрей від комах** (insect repellent)
sprej vid ko-MAKH

9) **озеро** (lake)
O-ze-ro

10) **рятувальник** (lifesaver/lifeguard)
r'a-tu-VAL'-nyk

11) **замок з піску** (sandcastle)
ZA-mok z pis-KU

12) **піти в похід** (to go on a hike)
pi-TY v po-HID

Мені більше подобається плавати в озері, ніж в басейні.
I prefer swimming in a lake over a swimming pool.

Не забудь взяти сонцезахисний крем, коли йдеш на пляж.
Don't forget to take sunscreen when you go to the beach.

Влітку він працює рятувальником.
He works as a lifeguard in summer.

QUIZ #2

Use arrows to match English words with their corresponding Ukrainian translations:

a. swim

b. wallet

c. crocodile

d. blossom

e. cold

f. rat

g. dress

h. bear

i. to get tanned

j. spider

k. sunny

l. snail

m. squirrel

n. jacket

o. monkey

p. butterfly

1. крокодил

2. метелик

3. павук

4. щур

5. білка

6. мавпа

7. ведмідь

8. равлик

9. куртка

10. сукня

11. гаманець

12. холодно

13. квітка

14. плавати

15. засмагати

16. сонячно

Fill in the blank spaces with the options below (use each word only once):

Цих вихідних мої друзі хочуть _____. Вони кажуть, що буде весело. Але мені не подобається ця ідея. Намети – це дискомфорт. Потрібно брати шорти, джинси, плащі, а я люблю сукні та _____. Буде сонячно та спекотно, а я не люблю таку погоду. Я люблю, коли _____. Так, там є _____, але я не люблю плавати. Я можу засмагати, якщо є _____, але недовго. Окрім того, я боюся комах: ґедзів, мух, _____! А дикі тварини? Кажани і _____! Ще мої друзі будуть їсти _____ з озера. Але я не люблю рибу! Напевно, я залишуся вдома.

озеро   прохолодно

спідниці   сонцезахисний крем

комарів   жити в наметах

вовки   рибу

ПОРИ РОКУ: ОСІНЬ (THE SEASONS – FALL/AUTUMN)

1) **опале листя** (fallen leaves)
   o-PA-le LYS-t'a

2) **згрібати листя** (to rake leaves)
   zhri-BA-ty LYS-t'a

3) **гарбуз** (pumpkin)
   har-BUZ

4) **вирізати гарбуз** (to carve a pumpkin)
   vy-ri-ZA-ty har-BUZ

5) **збирання яблук** (apple picking)
   zby-RAN'-n'a YAB-luk

6) **костюм на Гелловін** (Halloween costume)
   kos-T'UM na Hel-lo-VIN

7) **цукерки на Гелловін** (Halloween candy)
   tsu-KER-ky na Hel-lo-VIN

8) **ароматичні свічки** (scented candles)
   a-ro-ma-TYCH-ni SVICH-ky

9) **вечеря на День подяки** (Thanksgiving dinner)
   ve-CHE-r'a na den' po-D'A-ky

10) **вовняна ковдра** (wool blanket)
    VOV-n'a-na KOVD-ra

11) **смажити зефір** (to roast marshmallows)
    SMA-zhy-ty ze-FIR

12) **прикрашати сад** (to decorate the garden)
    pryk-ra-SHA-ty sad

Згрібати листя в саду восени – обов'язок наших дітей.
Raking leaves in the garden in autumn is our kids' duty.

Ми купили ароматичні свічки для холодних осінніх вечорів.
We bought scented candles for cold autumn nights.

Я подарую бабусі теплу вовняну ковдру.
I'll give my grandmother a warm wool blanket as a present.

ПОРИ РОКУ: ЗИМА (THE SEASONS – WINTER)

1) **гарячий шоколад** (hot cocoa/hot chocolate)
   ha-R'A-chyj sho-ko-LAD

2) **санки** (sled/sledge)
   SAN-ky

3) **рукавиці** (mittens)
   ru-ka-VY-tsi

4) **дута куртка** (puffy jacket)
   DU-ta KURT-ka

5) **суп** (soup)
   sup

6) **імбирне печиво** (gingerbread cookies)
   im-BYR-ne PE-chy-vo

7) **замерзле вікно** (frosty window)
   za-MERZ-le vik-NO

8) **соснова шишка** (pinecone)
   sos-NO-va SHYSH-ka

9) **катання на ковзанах** (ice skating)
   ka-TAN'-n'a na kov-za-NAKH

10) **катання на лижах** (skiing)
    ka-TAN'-n'a na LY-zhakh

11) **каток** (ice rink)
    ka-TOK

12) **сніжка** (snowball)
    SNIZH-ka

Бабуся зв'язала мені нові рукавиці.
My grandmother has knitted new mittens for me.

Чашка гарячого шоколаду – мій улюблений десерт взимку.
A cup of hot chocolate is my favorite winter dessert.

Час діставати мою дуту куртку з шафи.
It's time to get my puffy jacket out of the closet.

ЧАС (TIME)

1) **часовий пояс** (time zone)
   cha-so-VYJ PO-yas

2) **секунда** (second)
   se-KUN-da

3) **хвилина** (minute)
   hvy-LY-na

4) **година** (hour)
   ho-DY-na

5) **день** (day)
   den'

6) **тиждень** (week)
   TYZH-den'

7) **два тижні** (fortnight)
   dva TYZH-ni

8) **місяць** (month)
   MI-s'ats'

9) **рік** (year)
   rik

10) **світанок** (dawn)
    svi-TA-nok

11) **ранок** (morning)
    RA-nok

12) **опівдні** (noon/midday)
    o-PIV-dni

13) **день** (afternoon)
    den'

14) **сутінки** (dusk)
    SU-tin-ky

15) **ніч** (night)
    nich

16) **північ** (midnight)
    PIV-nich

17) **дата** (date)
    DA-ta

18) **календар** (calendar)
    ka-len-DAR

Рік закінчився, і мені потрібно купити новий календар.
The year is over, and I need to buy a new calendar.

Ти будеш вільна через дві години?
Will you be free in two hours?

Північ — чарівний час у казках.
Midnight is a magical time in fairy tales.

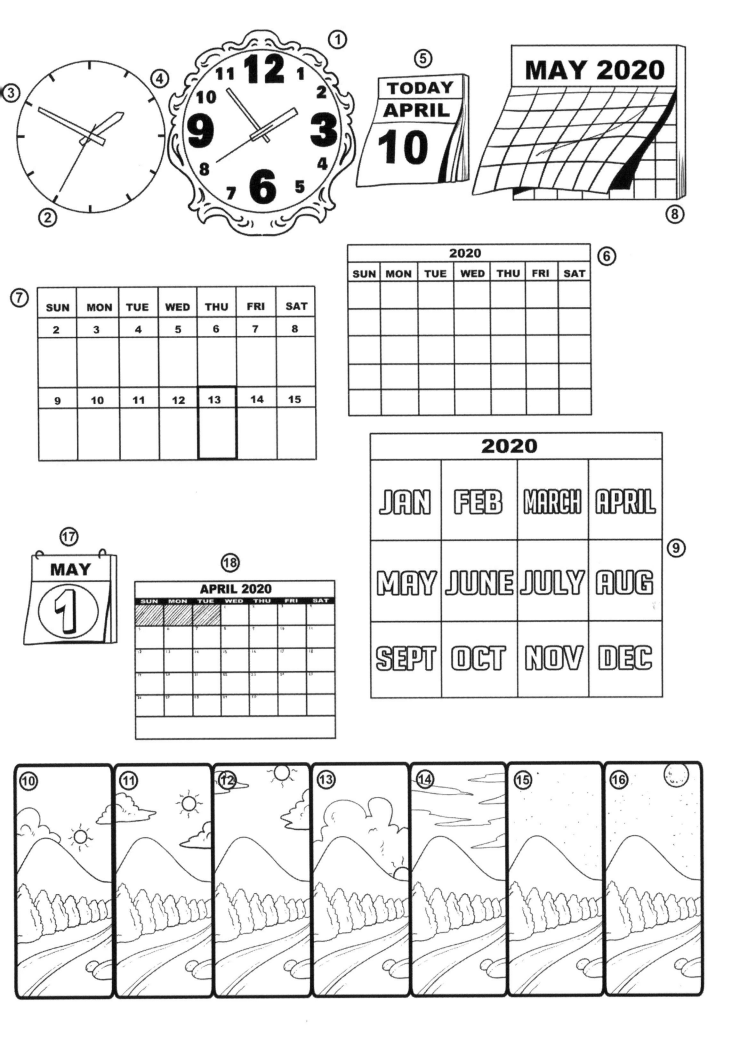

БУДИНОК/ДІМ (THE HOUSE)

1) **горище** (attic)
ho-RY-sche

2) **дах** (roof)
dakh

3) **стеля** (ceiling)
STE-l'a

4) **димохід** (chimney)
dy-mo-KHID

5) **стіна** (wall)
sti-NA

6) **балкон** (balcony)
bal-KON

7) **ґанок** (porch)
GA-nok

8) **вікно** (window)
vik-NO

9) **жалюзі** (shutters)
zha-l'u-ZI

10) **двері** (door)
DVE-ri

11) **сходи** (stairs)
SKHO-dy

12) **поруччя** (banister)
po-RUCH-cha

13) **підлога** (floor)
pid-LO-ha

14) **підвал** (basement)
pid-VAL

15) **подвір'я** (backyard)
pod-VI-r'ya

16) **гараж** (garage)
ha-RAZH

17) **під'їзд** (driveway)
pid-YIZD

18) **паркан** (fence/picket fence)
par-KAN

19) **поштова скринька** (mailbox)
posh-TO-va SKRYN'-ka

20) **коридор** (hallway/corridor)
ko-ry-DOR

У дитинстві ми вірили, що на горищі живуть привиди.
In our childhood, we used to believe that there were ghosts living in the attic.

Подвір'я наших сусідів таке брудне!
Our neighbors' backyard is so dirty!

Наше поруччя зламалось і нам потрібне нове.
Our banister is broken, and we need a new one.

КУХОННІ ПРЕДМЕТИ (KITCHEN ITEMS)

1) **плита** (stove)
ply-TA

2) **мікрохвильова піч** (microwave oven)
mik-ro-khvy-l'o-VA pich

3) **духовка** (oven)
du-HOV-ka

4) **електричний міксер** (electric mixer)
e-lek-TRYCH-nyj MIK-ser

5) **блендер** (blender)
BLEN-der

6) **тостер** (toaster oven)
TOS-ter

7) **кавоварка** (coffee maker)
ka-vo-VAR-ka

8) **холодильник** (fridge)
ho-lo-DYL'-nyk

9) **комора** (pantry)
ko-MO-ra

10) **кухонна шафка** (cupboard)
ku-HON-na SHAF-ka

11) **форма для торта** (cake pan)
FOR-ma dl'a tor-TA

12) **сковорода** (frying pan)
sko-vo-ro-DA

13) **каструля** (pot)
kas-TRU-l'a

14) **формочки для печива** (cookie cutters)
FOR-moch-ky dl'a PE-chy-va

15) **миска** (mixing bowl)
MYS-ka

16) **друшляк** (colander)
drush-L'AK

17) **сито** (strainer)
SY-to

18) **качалка** (rolling pin)
ka-CHAL-ka

19) **прихватка** (oven mitt)
PRYKH-vat-ka

20) **фартух** (apron)
FAR-tukh

Ти не приготуєш цей крем без електричного міксера.
You won't make this cream without an electric mixer.

Холодильник зовсім порожній. Треба йти за покупками!
The fridge is totally empty. It's time to go shopping!

Твоя комора схожа на магазин: тут є все!
Your pantry looks like a shop: you've got everything here!

ПРЕДМЕТИ В СПАЛЬНІ (BEDROOM ITEMS)

1) **ліжко** (bed)
LIZH-ko

2) **матрац** (mattress)
mat-RATS

3) **постільна білизна** (bedding/bed linen)
po-STIL'-na bi-LYZ-na

4) **подушка** (pillow)
po-DUSH-ka

5) **підковдра** (duvet cover)
pid-KOV-dra

6) **ковдра** (blanket)
KOV-dra

7) **простирадло** (sheet)
pros-ty-RAD-lo

8) **наволочка** (pillowcase)
NA-vo-loch-ka

9) **тумбочка** (nightstand)
TUM-boch-ka

10) **настільний годинник** (table clock)
na-STIL'-nyj ho-DYN-nyk

11) **настільна лампа** (table lamp)
na-STIL'-na LAM-pa

12) **шафа** (closet)
SHA-fa

13) **крісло-гойдалка** (rocking chair)
KRIS-lo HOJ-dal-ka

14) **лампа** (lamp)
LAM-pa

15) **дзеркало** (mirror)
DZER-ka-lo

16) **комод** (dresser)
ko-MOD

17) **занавіска** (curtain)
za-na-VIS-ka

18) **колиска** (cradle/crib)
ko-LYS-ka

19) **іграшки над колискою** (crib mobile)
IH-rash-ky nad ko-LYS-ko-yu

20) **вішак** (hanger)
vi-SHAK

Крісло-гойдалка займає занадто багато місця в цій кімнаті.
The rocking chair takes up too much space in this room.

Чиста і свіжа постільна білизна — це маленька життєва насолода.
Clean and fresh bed linen is one of life's little pleasures.

Цей вішак дуже зручний.
This hanger is very convenient.

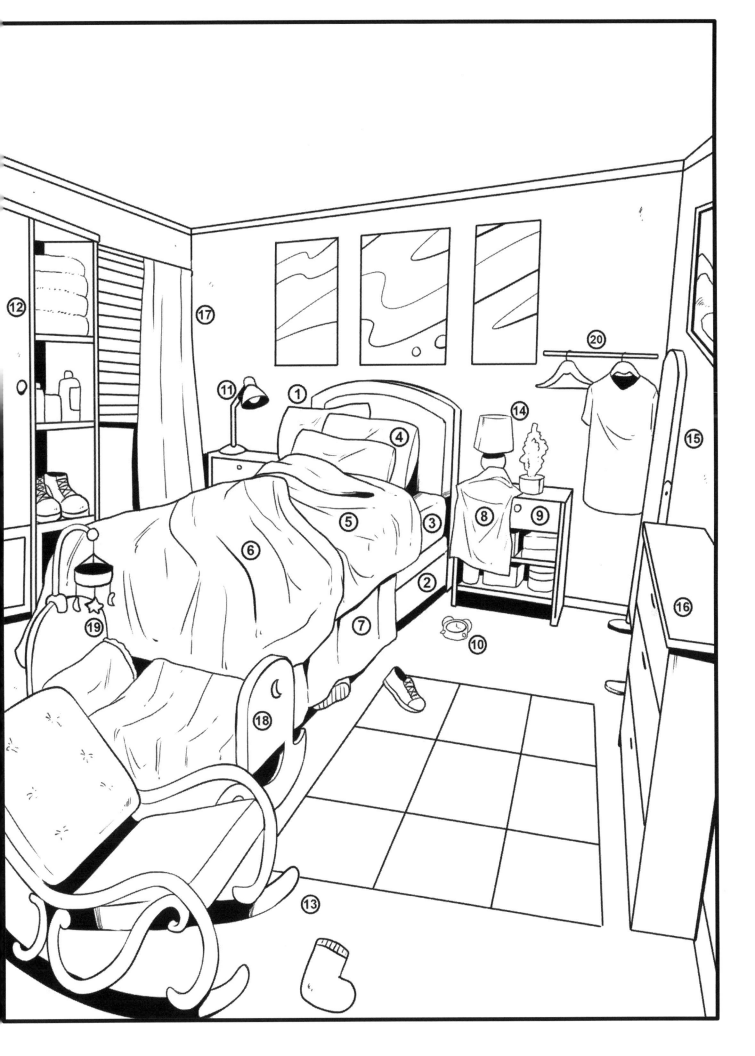

ПРЕДМЕТИ У ВАННІЙ КІМНАТІ (BATHROOM ITEMS)

1) **шторки для душу** (shower curtain)
SHTOR-ky dl'a DU-shu

2) **рушник** (towel)
rush-NYK

3) **вішак для рушників** (towel rack)
vi-SHAK dl'a rush-ny-KIV

4) **рушничок для рук** (hand towel)
rush-ny-CHOK dl'a ruk

5) **ванна** (bathtub)
VAN-na

6) **душ** (shower)
dush

7) **туалет** (toilet)
tu-a-LET

8) **раковина/умивальник** (sink/washbasin)
RA-ko-vy-na/u-my-VAL'-nyk

9) **кран** (faucet/tap)
kran

10) **килимок для ванної** (bath mat)
ky-ly-MOK dl'a VAN-no-yi

11) **аптечка** (medicine cabinet)
ap-TECH-ka

12) **зубна паста** (toothpaste)
zub-NA PAS-ta

13) **зубна щітка** (toothbrush)
zub-NA SCHI-tka

14) **шампунь** (shampoo)
sham-PUN'

15) **гребінець** (comb)
hre-bi-NETS'

16) **мило** (soap)
MY-lo

17) **піна для гоління** (shaving foam)
PI-na dl'a ho-LIN'-n'a

18) **бритва** (razor/shaver)
BRYT-va

19) **туалетний папір** (toilet paper)
tu-a-LET-nyj pa-PIR

20) **вантуз** (plunger)
VAN-tuz

21) **щітка для унітазу** (toilet brush)
SCHIT-ka dl'a u-ni-TA-zu

22) **кошик для сміття/смітник** (wastebasket)
KO-shyk dl'a smit-T'A/smit-NYK

Хто знову взяв мою зубну пасту?
Who took my toothpaste again?

Я не вмію користуватися вантузом.
I don't know how to use a plunger.

У тебе така чиста ванна! Яким миючим засобом ти користуєшся?
Your bathtub is so clean! What kind of detergent do you use?

ПРЕДМЕТИ У ВІТАЛЬНІ (LIVING ROOM ITEMS)

1) **меблі** (furniture)
MEB-li

2) **стілець** (chair)
sti-LETS'

3) **диван** (sofa)
dy-VAN

4) **кушетка** (couch)
ku-SHET-ka

5) **подушка** (cushion)
po-DUSH-ka

6) **журнальний столик** (coffee table)
zhur-NAL'-nyj STO-lyk

7) **попільничка** (ashtray)
po-pil'-NYCH-ka

8) **ваза** (vase)
VA-za

9) **прикраси** (decorations)
pryk-RA-sy

10) **книжкова полиця**
(bookshelf/bookcase)
knyzh-KO-va po-LY-ts'a

11) **тримач журналів** (magazine holder)
try-MACH zhur-NA-liv

12) **стерео** (stereo)
STE-re-o

13) **колонки** (speakers)
ko-LON-ky

14) **камін** (fireplace)
ka-MIN

15) **люстра** (chandelier)
L'UST-ra

16) **лампа** (lamp)
LAM-pa

17) **лампочка** (light bulb)
LAM-poch-ka

18) **настінний годинник** (wall clock)
na-STIN-nyj ho-DYN-nyk

19) **картина** (painting)
kar-TY-na

20) **телевізор** (TV/television)
te-le-VI-zor

21) **пульт** (remote control)
pul't

22) **ігрова приставка** (video game
console)
ih-ro-VA prys-TAV-ka

Усі меблі в цьому домі старовинні і дорогі.
All the furniture in this house is ancient and expensive.

Треба поміняти лампочку в люстрі.
We need to change the light bulb in the chandelier.

Ці подушки такі м'які! Я можу провести на них цілий день.
These cushions are so soft! I can spend all day on them.

ПРЕДМЕТИ В ЇДАЛЬНІ (DINING ROOM ITEMS)

1) **обідній стіл** (dining table)
   o-BID-nij stil

2) **скатертина** (tablecloth)
   ska-ter-TY-na

3) **центральний елемент** (centerpiece)
   tsent-RAL'-nyj e-le-MENT

4) **полотняна серветка** (cloth napkin)
   po-lot-N'A-na ser-VET-ka

5) **тарілка** (plate)
   ta-RIL-ka

6) **паперова серветка** (paper napkin)
   pa-pe-RO-va ser-VET-ka

7) **ніж** (knife)
   nizh

8) **виделка** (fork)
   vy-DEL-ka

9) **ложка** (spoon)
   LOZH-ka

10) **глечик** (pitcher/jug)
    HLE-chyk

11) **склянка/келих** (glass/goblet)
    SKL'AN-ka/KE-lykh

12) **кухоль/чашка** (mug/cup)
    KU-hol'/CHASH-ka

13) **сільничка** (saltshaker)
    sil'-NYCH -ka

14) **перечниця** (pepper shaker)
    PE-rech-ny-ts'a

15) **таця** (tray)
    TA-ts'a

16) **напій** (drink/beverage)
    na-PIJ

17) **їжа** (food)
    YI-zha

18) **закуска** (snack)
    za-KUS-ka

Я люблю закуски навіть більше, ніж основні страви.
I like snacks even more than main courses.

Передай мені сільничку, будь ласка.
Could you pass me the saltshaker, please?

Повечеряєш з нами?
Would you like to join us for dinner?

QUIZ #3

Use arrows to match English words with their corresponding Ukrainian translations:

a. sink

b. ashtray

c. oven

d. morning

e. tablecloth

f. pillow

g. week

h. fallen leaves

i. painting

j. bowl

k. pepper shaker

l. closet

m. porch

n. sledge

o. toothpaste

p. soup

1. ранок

2. тиждень

3. шафа

4. подушка

5. раковина

6. зубна паста

7. попільничка

8. санки

9. миска

10. перечниця

11. ганок

12. духовка

13. картина

14. скатертина

15. суп

16. опале листя

Fill in the blank spaces with the options below (use each word only once):

Цей рік найщасливіший у моєму житті: ми купили будинок! Ми переїжджаємо через _____. Біля будинку є великий _____ для нашого автомобіля. Перед будинком – великий _____. Тут я буду вкриватися вовняним пледом і читати книги. Відчинимо _____? Велика вітальня. Мені дуже подобається диван та _____. І, звичайно ж, _____ для моїх книг! У кухні є велика _____ і духовка. Тут я буду пекти _____. У їдальні – великий та широкий _____, якраз для нашої родини. У спальні є ліжко та _____, але він замаленький для моїх речей. У ванній кімнаті є _____, але немає ванни. Я дуже щаслива і не можу дочекатися переїзду!

два тижні

камін

обідній стіл

комора

ґанок

комод

двері

рік

імбирне печиво

книжкова полиця

душ

гараж

САД/ДВІР (THE GARDEN/THE BACKYARD)

1) **садівник** (gardener)
sa-div-NYK

2) **сарай** (shed)
sa-RAJ

3) **кущ** (bush)
kusch

4) **газон** (lawn)
ha-ZON

5) **трава** (grass)
tra-VA

6) **квітка** (flower)
KVIT-ka

7) **садовий шланг** (garden hose)
sa-DO-vyj shlanh

8) **лійка** (watering can)
LIJ-ka

9) **горщик для квітів** (flowerpot)
HOR-schyk dl'a KVI-tiv

10) **садові рукавички**
(gardening gloves)
sa-DO-vi ru-ka-VYCH-ky

11) **лопата** (shovel)
lo-PA-ta

12) **граблі** (rake)
HRAB-li

13) **садові вила** (garden fork)
sa-DO-vi VY-la

14) **секатор** (pruner/pruning shears)
se-KA-tor

15) **садовий шпатель** (garden trowel)
sa-DO-vyj SHPA-tel'

16) **кран** (tap)
kran

17) **тачка** (wheelbarrow)
TACH-ka

18) **газонокосарка** (lawn mower)
ha-zo-no-ko-SAR-ka

19) **ліхтарик** (lantern)
likh-TA-ryk

20) **лоза** (vine)
lo-ZA

Принеси лійку з сараю, будь ласка!
Can you bring the watering can from the shed, please?

Він може працювати в саду цілий день.
He can work in the garden all day long.

Чому ти працюєш без садових рукавичок?
Why are you working without your gardening gloves on?

ПРИБИРАННЯ (THE CLEANING ROOM)

1) **пральна машина** (washing machine)
PRAL'-na ma-SHY-na

2) **сушарка** (dryer)
su-SHAR-ka

3) **праска** (iron)
PRAS-ka

4) **прасувальна дошка** (ironing board)
pra-su-VAL'-na DOSH-ka

5) **господарське мило** (laundry soap)
hos-po-DARS'-ke MY-lo

6) **пральний порошок** (laundry detergent)
PRAL'-nyj po-ro-SHOK

7) **кондиціонер для білизни** (fabric softener)
kon-dy-tsi-o-NER dl'a bi-LYZ-ny

8) **кошик для білизни** (laundry basket)
KO-shyk dl'a bi-LYZ-ny

9) **брудний одяг** (dirty clothes)
brud-NYJ O-d'ah

10) **чиста білизна** (clean laundry)
CHYS-ta bi-LYZ-na

11) **мітла** (broom)
mit-LA

12) **совок** (dustpan)
so-VOK

13) **гумові рукавички** (rubber gloves)
HU-mo-vi ru-ka-VYCH-ky

14) **губка** (sponge)
HUB-ka

15) **тазик** (basin)
TA-zyk

16) **швабра** (mop)
SHVAB-ra

17) **відро** (bucket)
vid-RO

18) **ганчірки для чищення** (cleaning rags)
han-CHIR-ky dl'a CHY-schen'-n'a

19) **щітка** (scrub brush)
SCHIT-ka

20) **відбілювач** (bleach)
vid-BI-l'u-vach

21) **дезінфекційний засіб** (disinfectant)
dez-in-FEK-tsij-nyj

22) **відро для сміття** (trash can)
vid-RO dl'a smit'-T'A

Кошик для білизни знову повний.
The laundry basket is full again.

Відбілювач може зіпсувати одяг.
Bleach can ruin clothes.

Ти користуєшся кондиціонером для білизни?
Do you use a fabric softener?

ШКОЛА/УНІВЕРСИТЕТ (THE SCHOOL/THE UNIVERSITY)

1) **вчитель m. / вчителька f. /викладач m. / викладачка f.** (teacher)
VCHY-tel'/ VCHY-tel'-ka.   /vyk-la-DACH /vyk-la-DACH-ka

2) **учень m. / учениця f. / студент m. / студентка f.** (student)
U-chen'/ u-che-ny-TS'A
/stu-DENT / stu-DENT-ka

3) **клас** (classroom)
klas

4) **шафка** (locker)
SHAF-ka

5) **дошка оголошень** (bulletin board)
DOSH-ka o-ho-LO-shen'

6) **аркуш паперу** (sheet of paper)
AR-kush pa-PE-ru

7) **книга** (book)
KNY-ha

8) **блокнот** (notebook)
blok-NOT

9) **клей** (glue)
klej

10) **ножиці** (scissors)
NO-zhy-tsi

11) **олівець** (pencil)
o-li-VETS'

12) **гумка** (eraser)
HUM-ka

13) **підстругачка** (pencil sharpener)
pid-stru-HACH-ka

14) **ручка** (pen)
RUCH-ka

15) **маркер** (marker)
MAR-ker

16) **хайлайтер** (highlighter)
haj-LAJ-ter

17) **конверт** (envelope)
kon-VERT

18) **папка-планшет** (clipboard)
PAP-ka plan-SHET

19) **дошка** (blackboard)
DOSH-ka

20) **калькулятор** (calculator)
kal'-ku-L'A-tor

21) **лінійка** (ruler)
li-NIJ-ka

22) **степлер** (stapler)
STEP-ler

23) **пенал** (pencil case)
pe-NAL

24) **шкільна парта** (school desk)
shkil'-NA PAR-ta

25) **стіл** (table)
stil

26) **ноутбук** (laptop)
no-ut-BUK

Ти бачила список учнів на дошці оголошень?
Did you see the list of students on the bulletin board?

Я не користуюся калькулятором на уроках математики.
I don't use a calculator in math classes.

Діти, це ваш новий вчитель історії.
Kids, this is your new history teacher.

ОФІС (THE OFFICE)

1) **начальник** m. / **начальниця** f. (boss)
na-CHAL'-nyk / na-CHAL'-ny-ts'a

2) **керівник** m. / **керівниця** f. (head)
ke-riv-NYK / ke-riv-NY-ts'a

3) **працівник** m. / **працівниця** f. (employee)
pra-tsiv-NYK / pra-tsiv-NY-ts'a

4) **генеральний директор** m. / **генеральна директорка** f. (CEO/president)
he-ne-RAL'-nyj dy-REK-tor / he-ne-RAL'-na dy-REK-tor-ka

5) **бізнес-партнер** m. / **бізнес-партнерка** f. (business partner)
BIZ-nes part-NER / BIZ-nes part-NER-ka

6) **колега** (colleague)
ko-LE-ha

7) **співробітник** m. / **співробітниця** f.) (co-worker)/
spiv-ro-BIT-nyk / spiv-ro-BIT-ny-ts'a

8) **секретар** m. / **секретарка** f. (secretary)
sek-re-TAR / sek-re-TAR-ka

9) **кабінка** (cubicle)
ka-BIN-ka

10) **обертове крісло** (swivel chair)
o-ber-TO-ve KRIS-lo

11) **письмовий стіл** (desk)
pys'-MO-vyj stil

12) **комп'ютер** (computer)
kom-P'YU-ter

13) **принтер** (printer)
PRYN-ter

14) **канцелярське приладдя** (office supplies)
kan-tse-L'AR-s'ke pry-LAD-d'a

15) **печатка/штамп** (rubber stamp)
pe-CHAT-ka/shtamp

16) **диспенсер для скотча** (tape dispenser)
dys-PEN-ser dl'a SKOT-cha

17) **папка** (folder)
PAP-ka

18) **шафка для документів** (filing cabinet)
SHAF-ka dl'a do-ku-MEN-tiv

19) **факс** (fax)
faks

20) **телефон** (telephone)
te-le-FON

Наш начальник дуже чуйна людина.
Our boss is a very understanding person.

Вона працює менеджером у видавництві.
She works as a manager in a publishing house.

На його письмовому столі завжди безлад.
His desk is always a mess.

ПРОФЕСІЇ (PROFESSIONS/OCCUPATIONS)

1) **інженер m. / інженерка f.** (engineer)
   in-zhe-NER / in-zhe-NER-ka

2) **космонавт m. / космонавтка f.** (astronaut)
   kos-mo-NAVT / kos-mo-NAVT-ka

3) **пілот m. / пілотеса f.** (pilot)
   pi-LOT / pi-lo-TE-sa

4) **суддя m., f.** (judge)
   sud-D'A

5) **пожежник m. / пожежниця f.** (firefighter)
   po-ZHEZH-nyk / po-ZHEZH-ny-ts'a

6) **поліцейський m. / поліцейська f.** (police officer)
   po-li-TSEJS'-kyj / po-li-TSEJS'-ka

7) **шеф-кухар m. / шеф-кухарка f.** (chef)
   shef-KU-khar / shef-KU-khar-ka

8) **диригент m. / диригентка f.** (conductor)
   dy-ry-HENT / dy-ry-HENT-ka

9) **професор m. / професорка f.** (professor)
   pro-FE-sor / pro-FE-sor-ka

10) **танцюрист** m. . **/ танцюристка** f. (dancer)
    tan-ts'u-RYST/tan-ts'u-RYST-ka

11) **бізнесмен m. / бізнесвумен** f. (businessman/ businesswoman)
    biz-nes-MEN / biz-nes-VU-men

12) **дресирувальник m. / дресирувальниця f.** (animal trainer)
    dre-sy-ru-VAL'-nyk / dre-sy-ru-VAL'-ny-ts'a

Багато дітей мріють стати космонавтами.
Many kids dream of becoming astronauts.

Суддя був несправедливим.
The judge was unfair.

Я багато вчився, щоб стати **інженером.**
I studied a lot to become an engineer.

ТРАНСПОРТНІ ЗАСОБИ (MEANS OF TRANSPORT)

1) **велосипед** (bike/bicycle)
ve-lo-sy-PED

2) **мотоцикл** (motorcycle/motorbike)
mo-to-TSYKL

3) **снігохід** (snowmobile)
sni-ho-HID

4) **автомобіль** (car/automobile)
av-to-mo-BIL′

5) **автобус** (bus)
av-TO-bus

6) **вантажівка** (truck)
van-ta-ZHIV-ka

7) **метро** (subway)
met-RO

8) **поїзд** (train)
PO-yizd

9) **водний мотоцикл** (jet ski)
VOD-nyj mo-to-TSYKL

10) **човен** (boat)
CHO-ven

11) **круїзний лайнер** (cruise ship)
kru-YIZ-nyj LAJ-ner

12) **підводний човен** (submarine)
pid-VOD-nyj CHO-ven

13) **дирижабль** (airship/blimp)
dy-ry-ZHABL′

14) **повітряна куля** (hot air balloon)
po-VIT-r′a-na KU-l′a

15) **літак** (plane/airplane)
li-TAK

16) **вертоліт** (helicopter/chopper)
ver-to-LIT

17) **космічний корабель** (space shuttle)
kos-MICH-nyj ko-ra-BEL′

Ти поїдеш поїздом чи автобусом?
Will you go by train or by bus?

Ми виграли подорож на круїзному лайнері.
We've won a cruise ship voyage.

Мій дідусь – водій вантажівки.
My grandfather drives a truck.

ПЕЙЗАЖІ (LANDSCAPES)

1) **гора** (mountain)
ho-RA

2) **тропічний ліс** (tropical rainforest)
tro-PICH-nyj lis

3) **пустеля** (desert)
pus-TE-l'a

4) **вулкан** (volcano)
vul-KAN

5) **скеля** (cliff)
SKE-l'a

6) **пляж** (beach)
pl'azh

7) **ліс** (forest)
lis

8) **печера** (cave)
pe-CHE-ra

9) **гейзер** (geyser)
HEJ-zer

10) **водоспад** (waterfall/falls)
vo-do-SPAD

11) **річка** (river)
RICH-ka

12) **стародавні руїни** (ancient ruins)
sta-ro-DAV-ni ru-YI-ny

У пустелі колись йде сніг?
Does it ever snow in the desert?

Це озеро – найбільше в країні.
This lake is the biggest in the country.

Я ніколи не бачив вулкан.
I've never seen a volcano.

СПОРТ I (SPORTS I)

1) **стрільба з лука** (archery)
stril'-BA z LU-ka

2) **бокс** (boxing)
boks

3) **велоспорт** (cycling)
ve-lo-SPORT

4) **фехтування** (fencing)
feh-tu-VAN'-n'a

5) **футбол** (football/soccer)
fut-BOL

6) **регбі** (rugby)
REG-bi

7) **настільний теніс/пінг-понг**
(table tennis/ping-pong)
na-STIL'-nyj TE-nis /pin-PONH

8) **волейбол** (volleyball)
vo-lej-BOL

9) **важка атлетика** (weightlifting)
vazh-KA at-LE-ty-ka

10) **катання на ковзанах** (skating)
ka-TAN'-n'a na kov-za-NAKH

11) **паралімпійські види спорту**
(paralympic sports)
pa-ra-lim-PIJS'-ki VY-dy SPOR-tu

12) **бейсбол** (baseball)
bejs-BOL

13) **баскетбол** (basketball)
bas-ket-BOL

Я фанат баскетболу.
I'm a basketball fan.

Мені подобається дивитися фехтування по телевізору.
I like watching fencing on TV.

Паралімпійські види спорту заслуговують поваги.
Paralympic sports deserve respect.

СПОРТ II (SPORTS II)

1) **бадмінтон** (badminton)
bad-min-TON

2) **гімнастика** (gymnastics)
him-NAS-ty-ka

3) **веслування** (rowing)
ves-lu-VAN'-n'a

4) **спортивне скелелазіння**
(sport climbing)
spor-TYV-ne ske-le-LA-zin'-n'a

5) **серфінг** (surfing)
SER-finh

6) **теніс** (tennis)
TE-nis

7) **стрибки на батуті** (trampolining)
stryb-KY na ba-TU-ti

8) **реслінг/боротьба** (wrestling)
RES-linh/bo-rot'-BA

9) **лижний спорт** (skiing)
LYZH-nyj sport

10) **бобслей** (bobsled)
bob-SLEJ

11) **фігурне катання** (figure skating)
fi-HUR-ne ka-TAN'-n'a

12) **плавання** (swimming)
PLA-van'-n'a

13) **водне поло** (water polo)
VOD-ne PO-lo

14) **хокей** (hockey)
ho-KEJ

У Росії хокей дуже популярний.
Hockey is very popular in Canada.

Лижний спорт не для мене.
Skiing is not for me.

Пограймо в бадмінтон!
Let's go play badminton!

РІЗДВО (CHRISTMAS DAY)

1) **омела** (mistletoe)
o-ME-la

2) **гірлянда** (garland)
hir-L'AN-da

3) **різдвяна ялинка** (Christmas tree)
rizd-V'A-na ya-LYN-ka

4) **різдвяні прикраси**
(Christmas decorations)
rizd-V'A-ni pryk-RA-sy

5) **різдвяні подарунки**
(Christmas gifts/presents)
rizd-V'A-ni po-da-RUN-ky

6) **різдвяна вечеря** (Christmas dinner)
rizd-V'A-na ve-CHE-r'a

7) **льодяник** (lollipop/candy cane)
l'o-D'A-nyk

8) **Пряничний чоловічок**
(gingerbread man)
PR'A–nych–nyj cho-lo-VI-chok

9) **Різдвяний ельф** (Christmas elf)
rizd-V'A-nyj el'f

10) **різдвяний капелюх** (Christmas hat)
rizd-V'A-nyj ka-pe-L'UH

11) **Дід Мороз** (Santa Claus)
Did Mo-ROZ

12) **сани Діда Мороза** (Santa's sleigh)
SA-ny DI-da Mo-RO-za

13) **різдвяна зірка** (Christmas star)
rizd-V'A-na ZIR-ka

14) **сніговик** (snowman)
sni-ho-VYK

15) **свічки** (candles)
svich-KY

Маленькі діти вірять у Діда Мороза.
Little kids believe in Santa Claus.

Ми прикрасили будинок гірляндами.
We decorated the house with garlands.

Давай зліпимо сніговика!
Let's make a snowman!

QUIZ #4

Use arrows to match English words with their corresponding Ukrainian translations:

a. Christmas tree

b. judge

c. skating

d. boss

e. cliff

f. candles

g. teacher

h. truck

i. tennis

j. iron

k. animal trainer

l. shovel

m. swimming

n. desk

o. mountain

p. helicopter

1. свічки

2. різдвяна ялинка

3. дресирувальник

4. вертоліт

5. теніс

6. суддя

7. скеля

8. гора

9. праска

10. вчитель

11. лопата

12. письмовий стіл

13. вантажівка

14. плавання

15. катання на ковзанах

16. начальник

Fill in the blank spaces with the options below (use each word only once):

Мені 17 років. Прощавай, школо, прощавай, _____! Потрібно вибрати професію. _____ залишив під ялинкою великий гарний блокнот. Я беру блокнот, _____ і записую професії. Мені подобається спорт, особливо _____, але я не хочу займатися цим професійно. Може, фотограф? Я подорожуватиму і фотографуватиму пейзажі: водоспади, пустелі та _____. Або я стану _____! Хоча ні, це небезпечно. Я буду _____! Я сидітиму в офісі, і в мене буде багато працівників. Але офіс це нудно: комп'ютер, принтер, _____. Ні, бізнес не для мене. А, може, я буду пілотом? Але я боюся _____! Знаю! Я куплю _____ і полечу у подорож. Але я обіцяв допомогти мамі. У саду на мене чекає _____, а потім відро та _____. До зустрічі, блокноте!

Дід Мороз

пожежником

повітряну кулю

ручку

бізнесменом

швабра

боротьба

шкільна парто

літаків

газонокосарка

вулкани

папки

МУЗИЧНІ ІНСТРУМЕНТИ (MUSICAL INSTRUMENTS)

1) **акустична гітара** (acoustic guitar)
a-kus-TYCH-na hi-TA-ra

2) **електрогітара** (electric guitar)
e-LEK-tro hi-TA-ra

3) **бас-гітара** (bass guitar)
bas hi-TA-ra

4) **барабани** (drums)
ba-ra-BA-ny

5) **фортепіано** (piano)
for-te-pi-A-no

6) **труба** (trumpet)
tru-BA

7) **губна гармошка** (harmonica)
hub-NA har-MOSH-ka

8) **флейта** (flute)
FLEJ-ta

9) **кларнет** (clarinet)
klar-NET

10) **арфа** (harp)
AR-fa

11) **волинка** (bagpipes)
vo-LYN-ka

12) **віолончель** (cello)
vi-o-lon-CHEL'

13) **скрипка** (violin)
SKRYP-ka

14) **саксофон** (saxophone)
sak-so-FON

Я хочу навчитися грати на гітарі.
I want to learn to play the guitar.

Він грав на барабанах ще в школі.
He played the drums back at school.

Скрипка – складний інструмент.
The violin is a complex instrument.

ФРУКТИ (FRUITS)

1) **полуниця** (strawberry)
   po-lu-NY-ts'a

2) **папайя** (papaya)
   pa-PA-ya

3) **слива** (plum)
   SLY-va

4) **диня** (melon)
   DY-n'a

5) **кавун** (watermelon)
   ka-VUN

6) **банан** (banana)
   ba-NAN

7) **манго** (mango)
   MAN-ho

8) **персик** (peach)
   PER-syk

9) **малина** (raspberry)
   ma-LY-na

10) **апельсин** (orange)
    a-pel'-SYN

11) **лимон** (lemon)
    ly-MON

12) **ананас** (pineapple)
    a-na-NAS

13) **лайм** (lime)
    lajm

14) **виноград** (grapes)
    vy-no-HRAD

15) **вишня** (cherry)
    VYSH-n'a

16) **яблуко** (apple)
    YAB-lu-ko

17) **груша** (pear)
    HRU-sha

18) **грейпфрут** (grapefruit)
    hrejp-FRUT

19) **саусеп** (soursop)
    sa-u-SEP

20) **кокос** (coconut)
    ko-KOS

У неї алергія на полуницю.
She's allergic to strawberries.

Мені потрібні яблуки для торта.
I need apples for the cake.

Банани можна використовувати у випічці.
Bananas can be used in baking.

ОВОЧІ (VEGETABLES)

1) **цвітна капуста** (cauliflower)
tsvit-NA ka-PUS-ta

2) **спаржа** (asparagus)
SPAR-zha

3) **броколі** (broccoli)
BRO-ko-li

4) **капуста** (cabbage)
ka-PUS-ta

5) **артишок** (artichoke)
ar-ty-SHOK

6) **брюссельська капуста**
(Brussels sprout)
br'us-SEL'-s'ka ka-PUS-ta

7) **кукурудза** (corn)
ku-ku-RUD-za

8) **салат** (lettuce)
sa-LAT

9) **шпинат** (spinach)
shpy-NAT

10) **помідор** (tomato)
po-mi-DOR

11) **огірок** (cucumber)
o-hi-ROK

12) **цукіні** (zucchini)
tsu-KI-ni

13) **гриби** (mushrooms)
hry-BY

14) **рукола** (arugula)
RU-ko-la

15) **баклажан** (eggplant)
bak-la-ZHAN

16) **болгарський перець** (bell pepper)
bol-HARS'-kyj PE-re-ts'

17) **цибуля** (onion)
tsy-BU-l'a

18) **гарбуз** (pumpkin/squash)
har-BUZ

19) **картопля** (potato)
kar-TOP-l'a

20) **буряк листовий** (Swiss chard)
bu-R'AK lys-to-VYJ

Спаржа містить багато заліза.
Asparagus contains a lot of iron.

Я завжди плачу, коли ріжу цибулю.
I always cry when I cut onions.

Давай купимо помідори і огірки для салату.
Let's buy tomatoes and cucumbers for the salad.

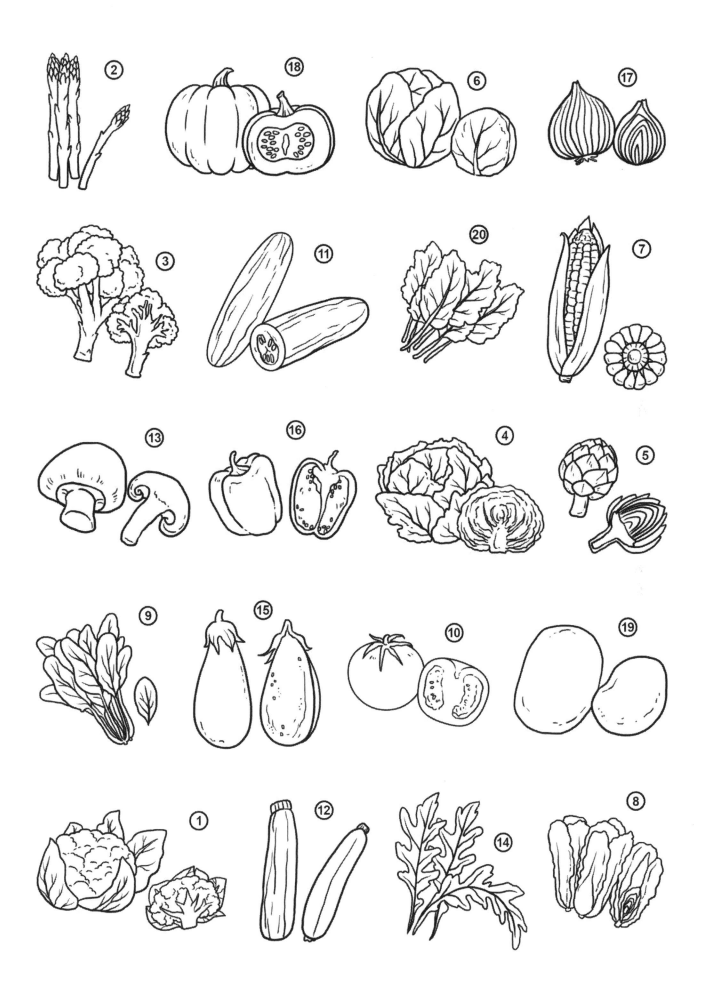

ТЕХНОЛОГІЇ (TECHNOLOGY)

1) **мобільний** (mobile)
   mo-BIL'-nyj

2) **прилад** (device)
   PRY-lad

3) **комп'ютер** (computer)
   kom-P'YU-ter

4) **веб-камера** (webcam)
   veb-KA-me-ra

5) **флешка** (flash drive)
   FLESH-ka

6) **жорсткий диск** (hard drive)
   zhorst-KYJ dysk

7) **карта пам'яті** (memory card)
   KAR-ta PA-m'ya-ti

8) **кард-рідер** (card reader)
   kard-RI-der

9) **бездротовий** (wireless, Wi-Fi)
   bez-dro-TO-vyj

10) **сонячна панель** (solar panel)
    SO-n'ach-na pa-NEL'

11) **принтер** (printer)
    PRYN-ter

12) **сканер** (scanner)
    SKA-ner

Тут є бездротовий інтернет?
Is there wireless internet here?

Мій мобільний розрядився
My mobile died.

Для роботи йому потрібна хороша веб-камера.
He needs a good webcam for his work.

НАУКА (SCIENCE)

1) **лабораторія** (laboratory)
   la-bo-ra-TO-ri-ya

2) **дослідник** (researcher)
   dos-LID-nyk

3) **розрахунки** (calculations)
   roz-ra-HUN-ky

4) **вчений** (scientist)
   VCHE-nyj

5) **лабораторний халат** (lab coat)
   la-bo-ra-TOR-nyj ha-LAT

6) **експеримент** (experiment)
   eks-pe-ry-MENT

7) **засоби особистого захисту** (personal protective equipment)
   ZA-so-by o-so-BYS-to-ho ZA-hys-tu

8) **тест** (test)
   test

9) **премія** (prize)
   PRE-mi-ya

10) **ризик** (risk)
    RY-zyk

11) **инструмент** (instrument)
    ins-tru-MENT

12) **статистика** (statistics)
    sta-TYS-ty-ka

Ви впевнені, що ці розрахунки правильні?
Are you sure that these calculations are correct?

Цей дослідник отримав Нобелівську премію.
This researcher has received the Nobel Prize.

Нам не вистачає засобів особистого захисту.
We're running short of personal protective equipment.

АСТРОНОМІЯ (ASTRONOMY)

1) **телескоп** (telescope)
te-les-KOP

2) **сонце** (sun)
SON-tse

3) **місяць** (moon)
MI-s'ats'

4) **галактика** (galaxy)
ha-LAK-ty-ka

5) **пояс астероїдів** (asteroid belt)
PO-yas as-te-RO-yi-div

6) **чорна діра** (black hole)
CHOR-na di-RA

7) **затемнення** (eclipse)
za-TEM-nen'-n'a

8) **летюча зірка** (shooting star)
le-T'U- cha ZIR-ka

9) **космічна станція** (space station)
kos-MICH-na STAN-tsi-ya

10) **білий карлик** (white dwarf)
BI-lyj KAR-lyk

11) **червоний гігант** (red giant)
cher-VO-nyj hi-HANT

12) **орбіта** (orbit)
or-BI-ta

13) **сузір'я** (constellation)
su-ZI-r'ya

14) **темна енергія** (dark energy)
TEM-na e-NER-hi-ya

15) **Плутон** (Pluto)
plu-TON

16) **туманність** (nebula)
tu-MAN-nist'

17) **Меркурій** (Mercury)
mer-KU-rij

18) **Венера** (Venus)
ve-NE-ra

19) **Земля** (Earth)
zem-L'A

20) **Марс** (Mars)
mars

21) **Юпітер** (Jupiter)
yu-PI-ter

22) **Сатурн** (Saturn)
sa-TURN

23) **Уран** (Uranus)
u-RAN

24) **Нептун** (Neptune)
nep-TUN

Я ніколи не бачив затемнення.
I've never seen an eclipse.

Подаруймо йому телескоп на день народження!
Let's give him a telescope for his birthday.

Дивися, це летюча зірка! Загадай бажання!
Look, it's a shooting star! Come on, make a wish!

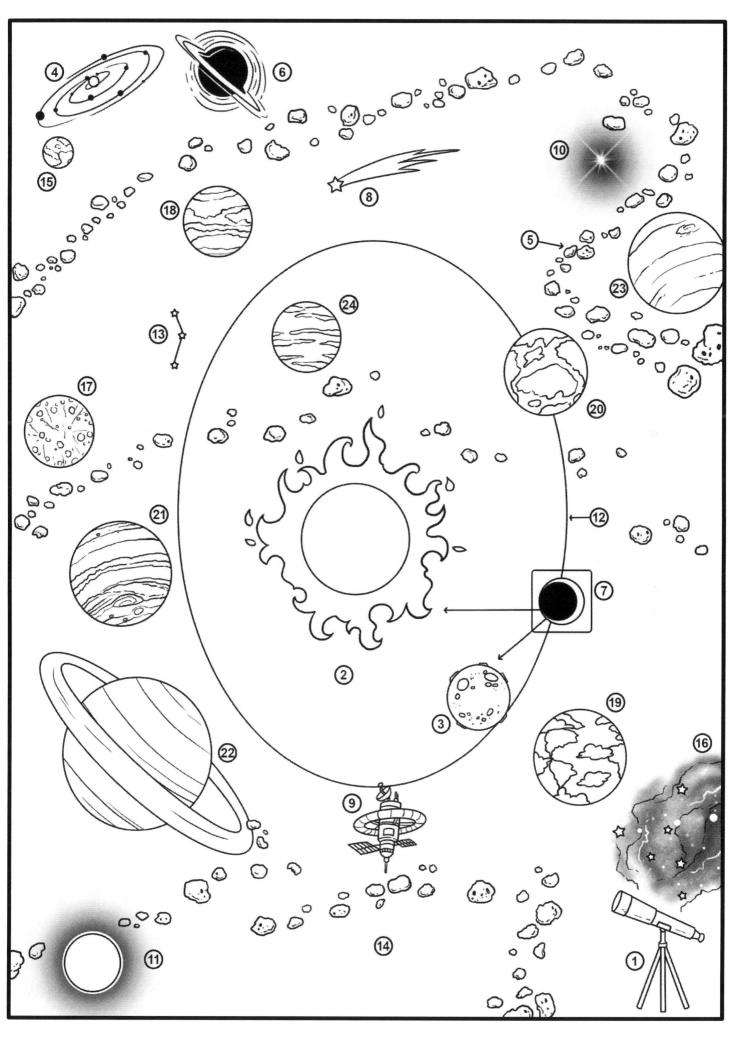

ГЕОГРАФІЯ (GEOGRAPHY)

1) **північ** (north)
PIV-nich

2) **схід** (east)
skhid

3) **південь** (south)
PIV-den'

4) **захід** (west)
ZA-hid

5) **екватор** (equator)
ek-VA-tor

6) **тропік Рака** (Tropic of Cancer)
TRO-pik RA-ka

7) **тропік Козерога** (Tropic of Capricorn)
TRO-pik ko-ze-RO-ha

8) **Південний полюс** (South Pole)
piv-DEN-nyj PO-l'us

9) **Північний полюс** (North Pole)
piv-NICH-nyj PO-l'us

10) **Полярне коло** (Arctic Circle)
po-L'AR-ne KO-lo

11) **континент** (continent)
kon-ty-NENT

12) **заморський** (overseas)
za-MORS'-kyj

13) **Африка** (Africa)
AF-ry-ka

14) **Азія** (Asia)
A-zi-ya

15) **Північна Америка** (North America)
piv-NICH-na a-ME-ry-ka

16) **Центральна Америка** (Central America)
tsent-RAL'-na a-ME-ry-ka

17) **Південна Америка** (South America)
piv-DEN-na a-ME-ry-ka

18) **Європа** (Europe)
yev-RO-pa

19) **Океанія** (Oceania)
o-ke-A-ni-ya

20) **Антарктида** (Antarctica)
an-tark-TY-da

21) **меридіан** (meridian)
me-ry-di-AN

22) **паралель** (parallel)
pa-ra-LEL'

23) **Атлантичний океан** (Atlantic Ocean)
at-lan-TYCH-nyj o-ke-AN

24) **Тихий океан** (Pacific Ocean)
TY-khyj o-ke-AN

Столиця знаходиться на півночі країни.
The capital is in the north of the country.

Ти знаєш, як Тихий океан отримав свою назву?
Do you know how the Pacific Ocean got its name?

Я мрію побачити Африку.
I dream of seeing Africa.

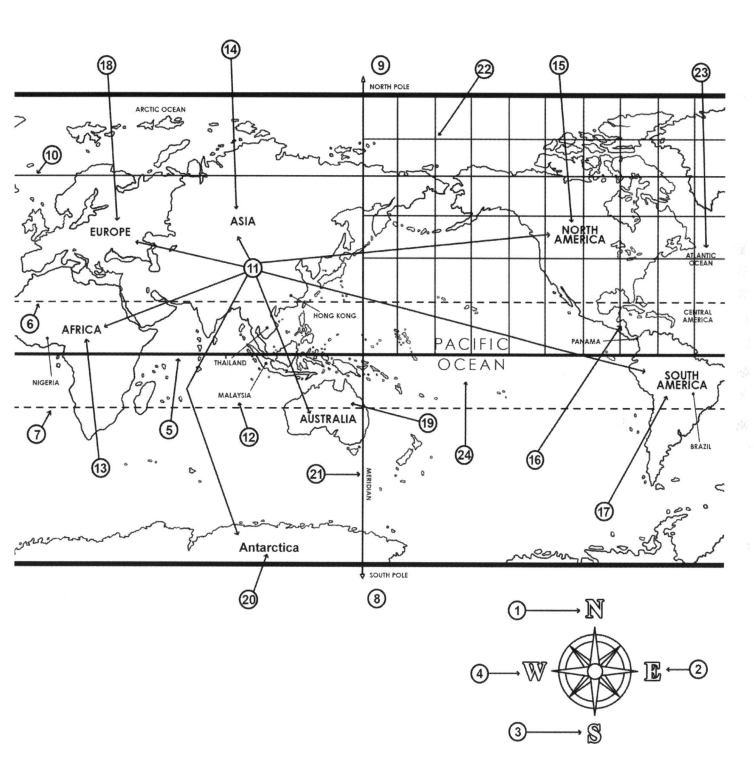

ЛІКАРНЯ (THE HOSPITAL)

1) **Лікар m./лікарка f./ медик m./медичка f.** (doctor/medic)
LI-kar/ LI-kar-ka/ME-dyk/ME-dych-ka

2) **медбрат m./медсестра f.** (nurse)
med-BRAT/med-sest-RA

3) **швидка допомога** (ambulance)
shvyd-KA do-po-MO-ha

4) **аптечка** (first aid kit)
ap-TECH-ka

5) **термометр** (thermometer)
ter-MO-metr

6) **ноші** (stretcher)
NO-shi

7) **шприц** (syringe)
shpryts

8) **голка** (needle)
HOL-ka

9) **стетоскоп** (stethoscope)
ste-to-SKOP

10) **милиці** (crutches)
MY-ly-tsi

11) **інвалідний візок** (wheelchair)
in-va-LID-nyj vi-ZOK

12) **оглядова кімната** (observation room)
oh-l'a-DO-va kim-NA-ta

13) **лікарняне ліжко** (hospital bed)
li-kar-N'A-ne LIZH-ko

14) **ін'єкція** (injection)
in-YEK-tsi-ya

15) **операція** (surgery)
o-pe-RA-tsi-ya

16) **історія хвороби** (medical history)
is-TO-ri-ya hvo-RO-by

17) **пацієнт** (patient)
pa-tsi-YENT

18) **пігулки/таблетки** (pills/tablets)
pi-HUL-ky/tab-LET-ky

Ці пігулки треба приймати перед їжею.
These pills should be taken before meals.

Ніколи не думав, що мені знадобляться милиці.
I never thought I would need crutches.

Операція тривала п'ять годин.
The surgery lasted five hours.

ФЕРМА (THE FARM)

1) **амбар** (barn)
am-BAR

2) **корівник/стайня** (cowshed/stable)
ko-RIV-nyk/STAJ-n'a

3) **фермер m./ фермерка f.** (farmer)
FER-mer/ FER-mer-ka

4) **плуг** (plow)
pluh

5) **силосна башта** (silo tower)
SY-los-na BASH-ta

6) **млин** (mill)
mlyn

7) **корито для води** (water trough)
ko-RY-to dl'a vo-DY

8) **курник** (henhouse)
kur-NYK

9) **вулик** (beehive)
VU-lyk

10) **тюк сіна** (hay bale)
t'uk SI-na'

11) **худоба** (cattle)
khu-DO-ba

12) **доїти** (to milk)
do-YI-ty

13) **стадо** (herd/flock)
STA-do

14) **курка** (hen)
KUR-ka

15) **колодязь** (well)
ko-LO-d'az'

16) **система зрошення**
(irrigation system)
sys-TE-ma ZRO-shen'-n'a

17) **опудало** (scarecrow)
o-PU-da-lo

18) **ґрунтова дорога** (dirt road)
grun-to-VA do-RO-ha

Птахи взагалі не бояться нашого опудала.
Birds are not afraid of our scarecrow at all.

Вчора на стадо нашого сусіда напав вовк.
A wolf attacked our neighbor's herd yesterday.

Ти вмієш доїти корів?
Can you milk cows?

QUIZ #5

Use arrows to match English words with their corresponding Ukrainian translations:

a. potato	1. худоба
b. sun	2. диня
c. melon	3. труба
d. nurse	4. Земля
e. flash drive	5. картопля
f. trumpet	6. вчений
g. mill	7. цибуля
h. device	8. медсестра
i. Earth	9. млин
j. syringe	10. захід
k. harp	11. сонце
l. onion	12. флешка
m. west	13. прилад
n. cattle	14. яблуко
o. apple	15. арфа
p. scientist	16. шприц

Fill in the blank spaces with the options below (use each word only once):

Я _____ і працюю в лабораторії. Мої друзі фермери і мешкають на _____ країни. Вони запросили мене у гості, і я з радістю погодився! Жодних комп'ютерів, веб-камер та інших _____. Лише свіже повітря, природа, корови і _____. А ще мої друзі вирощують овочі: картоплю, гарбузи та _____. Я купив екзотичні фрукти: папайю та _____. Ми зустрілися, пообідали, і мої друзі пішли доїти корів. Я хотів їм допомогти, але корова вдарила мене копитом прямо по голові! Я подумав, що це _____! В очах стало темно. Мої друзі викликали _____. Лікар сказав, що все добре. Увечері ми сиділи на ґанку і дивилися на _____. Мій друг грав на _____, і я забув про випадок із коровою.

сході   швидку допомогу

гітарі   кури

затемнення   вчений

помідори   ананас

місяць   приладів

ЇЖА (FOOD)

1) **родзинки** (raisins)
   rod-ZYN-ky

2) **волоські горіхи** (walnuts)
   vo-LOS'-ki ho-RI-khy

3) **м'ясо** (meat)
   M'YA-so

4) **баранина** (lamb)
   ba-RA-ny-na

5) **риба** (fish)
   RY-ba

6) **курка** (chicken)
   KUR-ka

7) **індичка** (turkey)
   in-DYCH-ka

8) **мед** (honey)
   med

9) **цукор** (sugar)
   TSU-kor

10) **сіль** (salt)
    sil'

11) **перець** (pepper)
    PE-rets'

12) **бекон** (bacon)
    be-KON

13) **сосиски** (sausages)
    so-SYS-ky

14) **кетчуп** (ketchup)
    KET-chup

15) **майонез** (mayonnaise)
    ma-yo-NEZ

16) **гірчиця** (mustard)
    hir-CHY-ts'a

17) **варення** (jam)
    va-REN'-n'a

18) **вершкове масло** (butter)
    versh-KO-ve MAS-lo

19) **сік** (juice)
    sik

20) **молоко** (milk)
    mo-lo-KO

Я вегетаріанець і не їм м'яса.
I am a vegetarian and don't eat meat.

У цьому супі забагато солі.
There is too much salt in this soup.

Будь ласка, не забудь купити рибу!
Please, don't forget to buy fish!

СТРАВИ (DISHES)

1) **лазанья** (lasagna)
la-ZAN'-ya

2) **картопляний омлет** (potato omelette)
kar-top-L'A-nyj om-LET

3) **м'ясний рулет** (meatloaf)
m'yas-NYJ ru-LET

4) **смажена локшина** (fried noodles)
SMA-zhe-na LOK-shy-na

5) **макарони з сиром** (macaroni and cheese)
ma-ka-RO-ny z SY-rom

6) **паелья** (paella)
pa-EL'-ya

7) **реберця барбекю** (barbecue ribs)
re-BER-ts'a bar-be-K'U

8) **кукурудзяний хліб** (cornbread)
ku-ku-RUD-z'a-nyj khlib

9) **спрінг-роли** (spring rolls)
sprinh-RO-ly

10) **чізбургер** (cheeseburger)
CHIZ-bur-her

11) **смажена курка** (fried chicken)
SMA-zhe-na KUR-ka

12) **салат Цезар** (Caesar salad)
sa-LAT TSE-zar

13) **цибулевий суп** (onion soup)
tsy-BU-le-vyj sup

14) **салат з капусти** (coleslaw)
sa-LAT z ka-PUS-ty

15) **гострі курячі крильця** (spicy chicken wings)
HOS-tri KU-r'a-chi KRYL'-ts'a

16) **шоколадне печиво** (chocolate chip cookies)
sho-ko-LAD-ne PE-chy-vo

17) **лаймовий пиріг** (key lime pie)
LAJ-mo-vyj py-RIH

18) **чізкейк** (cheesecake)
chiz-KEJK

Замовмо цибульний суп і макарони з сиром!
Let's order some onion soup and macaroni with cheese!

Можеш поділитися зі мною своїм рецептом шоколадного печива?
Can you share your chocolate chip cookie recipe with me?

Я на дієті, але не можу встояти перед куркою барбекю.
I'm on a diet, but I can't resist barbecue chicken.

МОРЕПРОДУКТИ (SEAFOOD)

1) **анчоус** (anchovy)
an-CHO-us

2) **тріска** (cod)
tris-KA

3) **краб-павук** (spider crab)
krab pa-VUK

4) **скумбрія** (mackerel)
SKUM-bri-ya

5) **лобстер** (lobster)
LOB-ster

6) **гребінець** (scallop)
hre-bi-NETS'

7) **луціан** (snapper)
l'u-tsi-AN

8) **лососева ікра/червона ікра**
(salmon roe)
lo-SO-se-va ik-RA/cher-VO-na ik-RA

9) **краб** (crab)
krab

10) **устриці** (oysters)
US-try-tsi

11) **вугор** (eel)
vu-HOR

12) **креветки** (shrimp)
kre-VET-tky

Тобі не здається, що ці креветки занадто дорогі?
Don't you think that these shrimps are too expensive?

Скумбрія – дуже жирна риба.
Mackerel is a very fatty fish.

Давай приготуємо бутерброди з червоною ікрою!
Let's make sandwiches with salmon roe!

ФОРМИ (SHAPES)

1) **коло** (circle)
KO-lo

2) **овал** (oval)
o-VAL

3) **трикутник** (triangle)
try-KUT-nyk

4) **прямокутник** (rectangle)
pr'a-mo-KUT-nyk

5) **квадрат** (square)
kvad-RAT

6) **трапеція** (trapezoid)
tra-PE-tsi-ya

7) **ромб** (rhombus)
romb

8) **куб** (cube)
kub

9) **п'ятикутник** (pentagon)
p'ya-ty-KUT-nyk

10) **шестикутник** (hexagon)
shes-ty-KUT-nyk

11) **стрілка** (arrow)
STRIL-ka

12) **хрест** (cross)
khrest

13) **серце** (heart)
SER-tse

14) **зірка** (star)
ZIR-ka

15) **циліндр** (cylinder)
tsy-LINDR

16) **конус** (cone)
KO-nus

17) **піраміда** (pyramid)
pi-ra-MI-da

18) **сфера** (sphere)
SFE-ra

19) **призма** (prism)
PRYZ-ma

Серце – символ кохання.
The heart is the symbol of love.

Мені подобається візерунок з трикутників на твоєму светрі.
I like the triangle pattern on your sweater.

Я купила своєму племіннику іграшкову піраміду.
I bought my nephew a toy pyramid.

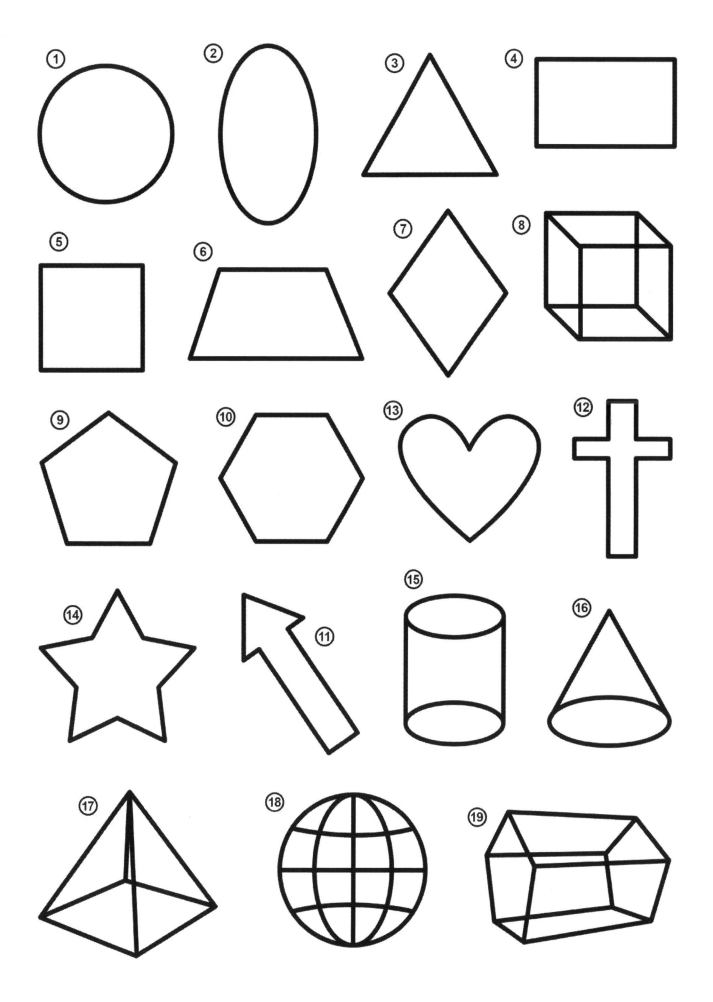

СУПЕРМАРКЕТ (THE SUPERMARKET)

1) **візок для покупок** (shopping cart)
vi-ZOK dl'a po-KU-pok

2) **вітрина** (cabinet/display case)
vit-RY-na

3) **покупець** (customer)
po-ku-PETS'

4) **касир** (cashier)
ka-SYR

5) **чек** (receipt)
chek

6) **пекарня** (bakery)
pe-KAR-n'a

7) **фрукти і овочі** (fruits and vegetables)
FRUK-ty i O-vo-chi

8) **м'ясо** (meat)
M'YA-so

9) **молочні продукти** (dairy products)
mo-LOCH-ni pro-DUK-ty

10) **риба** (fish)
RY-ba

11) **заморожені продукти** (frozen food)
za-mo-RO-zhe-ni pro-DUK-ty

12) **курятина** (poultry)
KU-r'a-ty-na

13) **бобові** (legumes)
bo-BO-vi

14) **закуски** (snacks)
za-KUS-ky

15) **десерт** (dessert)
de-SERT

16) **напої** (drinks)
na-PO-yi

17) **побутові предмети** (household items)
po-bu-TO-vi pred-ME-ty

18) **стрічковий конвеєр** (belt conveyor)
strich-ko-VYJ kon-VE-yer

Мій візок переповнений продуктами та побутовими предметами.
My cart is full of groceries and household items.

Моя тітка працює касиром у супермаркеті.
My aunt works as a cashier at a supermarket.

Взимку я купую заморожені овочі частіше, ніж свіжі.
In winter, I buy frozen vegetables more often than fresh ones.

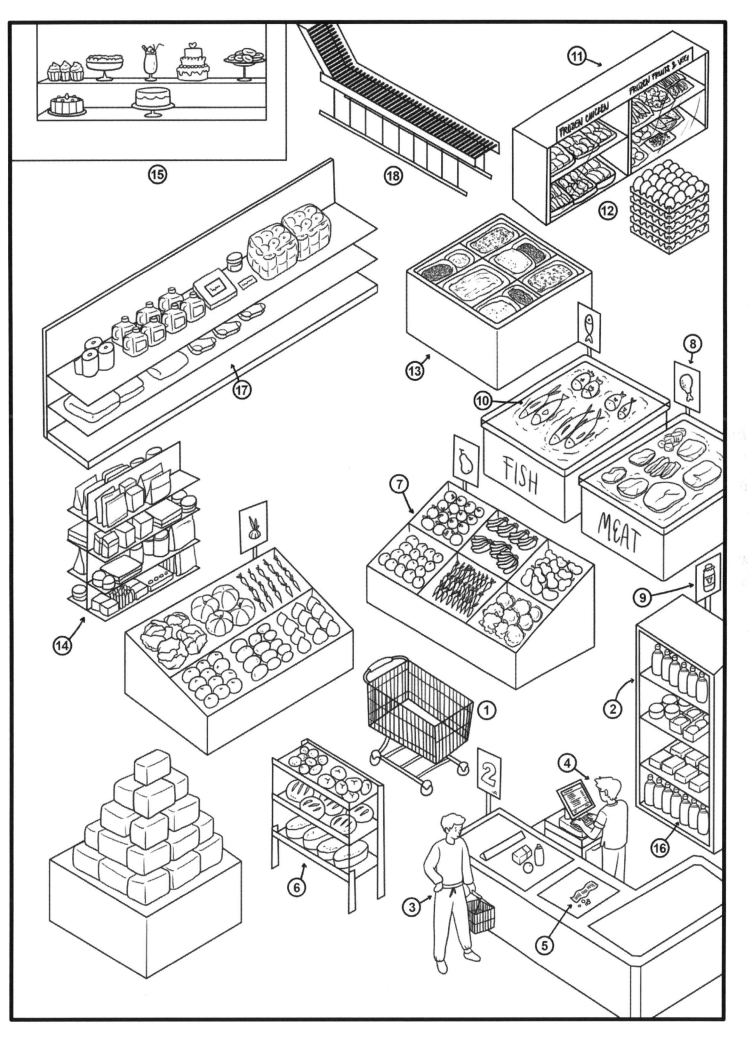

МЕДІА (MEDIA)

1) **журнал** (magazine)
   zhur-NAL

2) **факс** (fax)
   faks

3) **газета** (newspaper/journal)
   ha-ZE-ta

4) **пошта/кореспонденція** (postal mail)
   POSH-ta/ko-res-pon-DEN-tsi-ya

5) **лист** (letter)
   lyst

6) **радіо** (radio)
   RA-di-o

7) **комікс** (comic)
   KO-miks

8) **книга** (book)
   KNY-ha

9) **фотографія** (photography)
   fo-to-HRA-fi-ya

10) **стаціонарний телефон** (landline phone)
    sta-tsy-o-NAR-nyj te-le-FON

11) **телевізор** (TV)
    te-le-VI-zor

12) **фільми** (movies)
    FIL'-my

13) **мобільний телефон** (mobile/cell phone)
    mo-BIL'-nyj te-le-FON

14) **мова жестів** (sign language)
    MO-va ZHES-tiv

Я вивчив мову жестів, щоб розуміти свого німого друга.
I learned sign language to understand my mute friend.

Хтось ще користується стаціонарним телефоном?
Does anyone still use the landline phone?

Мій син витрачає купу грошей на комікси.
My son spends tons of money on comics.

ЯРМАРОК/ПАРК РОЗВАГ (THE FAIR/THE AMUSEMENT PARK)

1) **кімната сміху** (house of mirrors)
kim-NA-ta SMI-hu

2) **піратський корабель/човен**
(pirate ship/boat swing)
pi-RATS'-kyj ko-ra-BEL'/CHO-ven

3) **каса** (ticket booth)
KA-sa

4) **ланцюгова карусель** (swing ride)
lan-ts'u-HO-va ka-ru-SEL'

5) **американські гірки** (roller coaster)
a-me-ry-KAN-sk'i HIR-ky

6) **колесо огляду** (ferris wheel)
KO-le-so OH-l'a-du

7) **карусель** (carousel/merry-go-round)
ka-ru-SEL'

8) **автодром** (bumper cars)
av-to-DROM

9) **чашки** (teacups/cup and saucer)
chash-KY

10) **маятник** (pendulum)
MA-yat-nyk

11) **ігрові автомати** (arcade room)
ih-ro-VI av-to-MA-ty

12) **корн-дог** (corn dog)
korn-DOH

13) **морозиво** (ice cream)
mo-RO-zy-vo

14) **цукрова вата** (cotton candy)
tsuk-RO-va VA-ta

15) **яблуко в карамелі** (candy apple)
YAB-lu-ko v ka-ra-ME-li

Я боюся кататися на колесі огляду.
I'm afraid of riding a ferris wheel.

Я куплю квитки, а ти купи нам морозиво.
I'll go buy tickets, and you go and buy us ice cream.

Більш за все дітям сподобався автодром.
Kids liked the bumper cars most of all.

ЖИТТЄВІ ПОДІЇ (LIFE EVENTS)

1) **народження** (birth)
na-ROD-zhen'-n'a

2) **хрестини** (christening/baptism)
khres-TY-ny

3) **перший день у школі**
(first day of school)
PER-shyj den' u SHKO-li

4) **подружитися** (make friends)
po-dru-ZHY-ty-s'a

5) **день народження** (birthday)
den' na-ROD-zhen'-n'a

6) **закохатися** (fall in love)
za-ko-HA-ty-s'a

7) **закінчення школи** (graduation)
za-KIN-chen'-n'a SHKO-ly

8) **вступити до університету** (go to
university/college)
vstu-PY-ty do u-ni-ver-sy-TE-tu

9) **отримати роботу** (get a job)
ot-RY-ma-ty ro-BO-tu

10) **стати підприємцем** (become an
entrepreneur)
STA-ty pid-pry-YEM-tsem

11) **подорожувати по всьому світу**
(travel around the world)
po-do-ro-zhu-VA-ty po VS'O-mu SVI-
tu

12) **одружитися/вийти заміж**
(get married)
od-ru-ZHY-ty-s'a/VYJ-ty ZA-mizh

13) **народити дитину** (have a baby)
na-ro-DY-ty dy-TY-nu

14) **святкувати день народження**
(celebrate a birthday)
sv'at-ku-VA-ty den' na-ROD-zhen'-n'a

15) **вихід на пенсію** (retirement)
VY-hid na PEN-si-yu

16) **смерть** (death)
smert'

Народження дитини — найзахопливіша подія в моєму житті.
Having a baby is the most exciting event in my life.

Мій син хоче стати підприємцем.
My son wants to become an enterpreneur.

Вони подружилися в школі.
They became friends at school.

ПРИКМЕТНИКИ I (ADJECTIVES I)

1) **великий** (big)
   ve-LY-kyj

2) **маленький** (small)
   ma-LEN'-kyj

3) **гучний** (loud)
   huch-NYJ

4) **тихий** (silent)
   TY-khyj

5) **довгий** (long)
   DOV-hyj

6) **короткий** (short)
   ko-ROT-kyj

7) **широкий** (wide)
   shy-RO-kyj

8) **вузький** (narrow)
   vuz'-KYJ

9) **дорогий** (expensive)
   do-ro-HYJ

10) **дешевий** (cheap)
    de-SHE-vyj

11) **швидкий** (fast)
    shvyd-KYJ

12) **повільний** (slow)
    po-VIL'-nyj

13) **порожній** (empty)
    po-ROZH-nij

14) **повний** (full)
    POV-nyj

15) **м'який** (soft)
    m'ya-KYJ

16) **твердий** (hard)
    tver-DYJ

17) **високий** (tall)
    vy-SO-kyj

18) **низький** (short)
    nyz'-KYJ

Ця склянка повна. Дай мені порожню, будь ласка!
This glass is full. Give me an empty one, please.

Чому ти такий повільний?
Why are you so slow?

Ми купили великий будинок.
We've bought a big house.

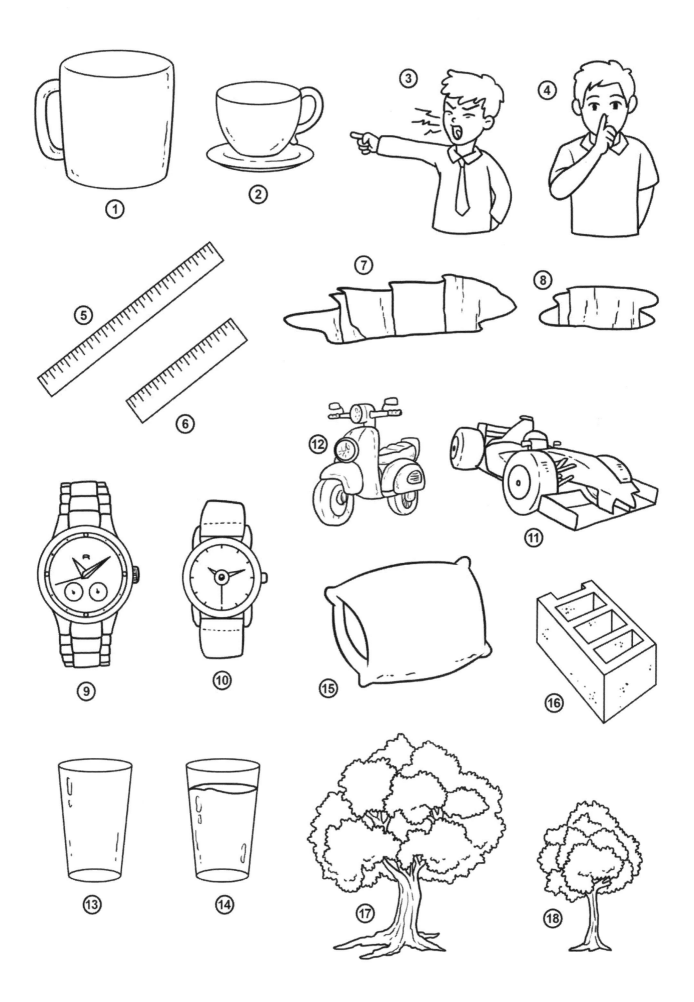

QUIZ #6

Use arrows to match English words with their corresponding Ukrainian translations:

a. fried chicken

b. cod

c. shopping cart

d. honey

e. magazine

f. meat

g. arrow

h. death

i. shrimp

j. circle

k. jam

l. book

m. house of mirrors

n. coleslaw

o. fast

p. big

1. візок для покупок

2. коло

3. салат з капусти

4. великий

5. кімната сміху

6. смажена курка

7. креветки

8. книга

9. журнал

10. смерть

11. варення

12. тріска

13. швидкий

14. м'ясо

15. мед

16. стрілка

Fill in the blank spaces with the options below (use each word only once):

Сьогодні свято – мій _____. Я не хотів гучного свята, просто _____ вечора вдома. Я замовив устриць та _____ і хотів просто сидіти вдома та дивитися _____. Але зранку прийшли мої батьки. Тато подарував мені _____, а мама спекла розкішний _____ – торт у формі _____ з родзинками та _____. Ще вона приготувала мій улюблений _____.

Потім прийшли мої друзі, і ми пішли до парку розваг. Ми каталися на _____, їли _____ і розважалися на _____. Це був чудовий день народження! Краще, ніж сидіти вдома та дивитися фільм!

тихого	серця
мобільний телефон	лобстера
день народження	колесі огляду
цукрову вату	ігрових автоматах
м'ясний рулет	фільм
десерт	волоськими горіхами

ПРИКМЕТНИКИ II (ADJECTIVES II)

1) **новий** (new)
no-VYJ

2) **старий** (old)
sta-RYJ

3) **зручний** (comfortable)
ZRUCH-nyj

4) **незручний** (uncomfortable)
ne-ZRUCH-nyj

5) **небезпечний** (dangerous)
ne-bez-PECH-nyj

6) **дратівливий** (annoying)
dra-tiv-LY-vyj

7) **хиткий** (shaky)
khyt-KYJ

8) **повний** (complete)
POV-nyj

9) **неповний** (incomplete)
ne-POV-nyj

10) **зламаний** (broken)
ZLA-ma-nyj

11) **чудовий** (gorgeous)
chu-DO-vyj

12) **віртуозний** (virtuous)
vir-tu-OZ-nyj

13) **схожий** (similar)
SHO-zhyj

14) **різний/інший** (different)
RIZ-nyj/IN-shyj

15) **відчинений** (open)
vid-CHY-ne-nyj

16) **зачинений** (closed)
za-CHY-ne-nyj

Моя колекція неповна без цієї марки.
My collection is incomplete without this stamp.

Ці старі чоботи зручніші, ніж нові.
These old boots are more comfortable than the new ones.

Навіщо тобі ця зламана іграшка?
Why do you need this broken toy?

ПРИСЛІВНИКИ (ADVERBS)

1) **тут** (here)
   tut

2) **там** (there)
   tam

3) **поруч/біля** (near)
   PO-ruch/BI-l'a

4) **далеко** (far)
   da-LE-ko

5) **вгорі** (up)
   VHO-ri

6) **внизу** (down)
   vny-ZU

7) **всередині** (inside)
   vse-RE-dy-ni

8) **зовні** (outside)
   ZOV-ni

9) **попереду** (ahead)
   po-PE-re-du

10) **позаду/за** (behind)
    po-ZA-du/za

11) **ні** (no)
    ni

12) **так** (yes)
    tak

13) **зараз** (now)
    ZA-raz

14) **добре/правильно** (well/good/right)
    DOB-re/ PRA-vyl'no

15) **погано/неправильно** (bad/wrong)
    po-HA-no/ne-PRA-vyl'no

Хто це за тобою?
Who is that behind you?

Я живу біля ріки.
I live near the river.

Що ти робиш сьогодні ввечері?
What are you doing tonight?

НАПРЯМКИ (DIRECTIONS)

1) **багатоквартирний будинок**
   (apartment building)
   ba-ha-to-kvar-TYR-nyj bu-DY-nok

2) **площа** (square)
   PLO-scha

3) **парк** (park)
   park

4) **метро** (subway)
   met-RO

5) **куток/поворот** (corner)
   ku-TOK/po-vo-ROT

6) **авеню** (avenue)
   a-ve-N'U

7) **вулиця** (street)
   VU-ly-ts'a

8) **автобусна зупинка** (bus stop)
   av-TO-bus-na zu-PYN-ka

9) **світлофор** (traffic lights)
   svit-lo-FOR

10) **пішохідний перехід**
    (crossing/crosswalk)
    pi-sho-KHID-nyj pe-re-KHID

11) **вгору** (up)
    VHO-ru

12) **вниз** (down)
    vnyz

13) **ліворуч/зліва** (left)
    li-VO-ruch/ZLI-va

14) **праворуч/справа** (right)
    pra-VO-ruch/SPRA-va

15) **дорожні знаки** (road signs)
    do-ROZH-ni ZNA-ky

16) **дорожня поліція/ДАІ**
    (traffic police)
    do-RO-zhn'a po-LI-tsi-ya/ da-I

Ідіть цією вулицею і поверніть ліворуч.
Go down the street and turn left.

Світлофор на повороті зламався.
The traffic lights on the corner are broken.

Що означає цей дорожній знак?
What does this road sign mean?

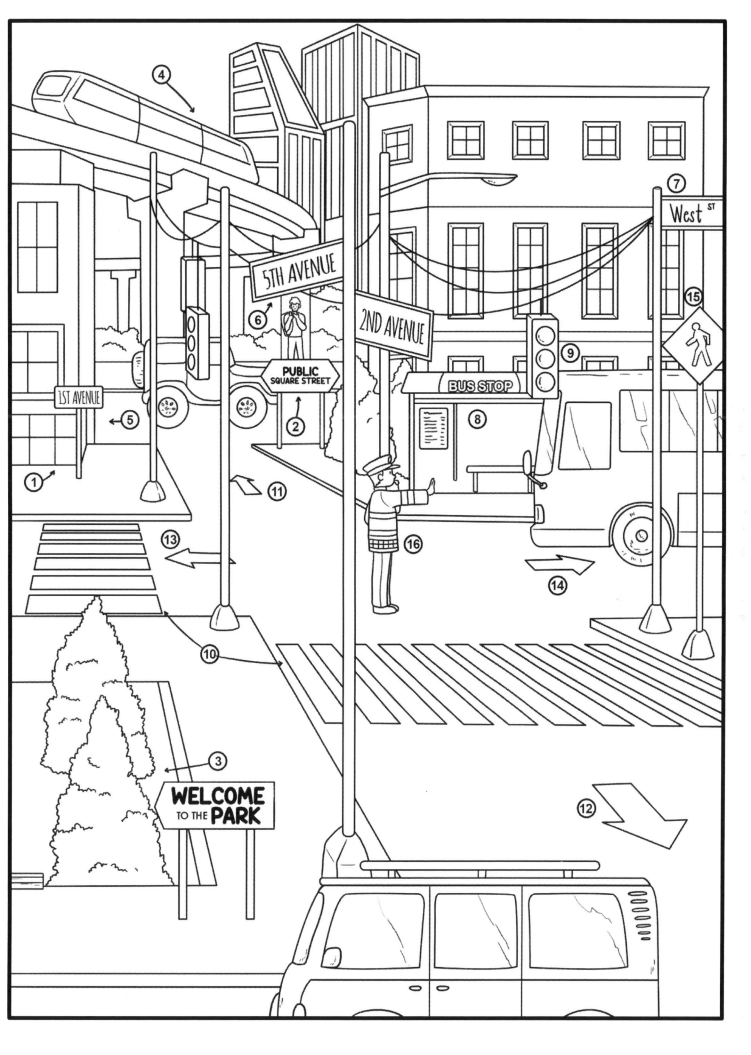

РЕСТОРАН (THE RESTAURANT)

1) **Менеджер m./менеджерка f.**
(manager)
ME-ne-dzher/ ME-ne-dzher-ka

2) **стіл** (table)
stil

3) **меню** (menu)
me-N'U

4) **страва** (dish)
STRA-va

5) **закуска** (appetizer)
za-KUS-ka

6) **перша страва** (starter)
PER-sha STRA-va

7) **основна страва** (main course)
os-nov-NA STRA-va

8) **десерт** (dessert)
de-SERT

9) **вечеря** (dinner)
ve-CHE-r'a

10) **кухар m./кухарка f.** (cook)
KU-khar/ ku-KHAR-ka

11) **офіціант** (waiter)
o-fi-tsi-ANT

12) **офіціантка** (waitress)
o-fi-tsi-ANT-ka

13) **чайові** (tip)
cha-yo-VI

14) **високий стілець** (high chair)
vy-SO-kyj sti-LETS'

15) **винна карта** (wine list)
VYN-na KAR-ta

16) **кондитер m./ кондитерка f.** (pastry chef)
kon-DY-ter/kon-DY-ter-ka

Скільки залишимо чайових?
How much shall we leave as a tip?

Моя мама працює кондитером у кафе.
My mother works as a pastry chef in a café.

Офіціанте, принесіть нам меню, будь ласка.
Waiter, bring us the menu, please.

ТОРГОВИЙ ЦЕНТР (THE MALL)

1) **поверх** (floor)
PO-verh

2) **акваріум** (aquarium)
ak-VA-ri-um

3) **фуд-корт** (food court)
fud-KORT

4) **ліфт** (elevator)
lift

5) **ескалатори** (escalators)
es-ka-LA-to-ry

6) **аварійний вихід** (emergency exit)
a-va-RIJ-nyj VY-khid

7) **салон краси** (beauty salon)
sa-LON kra-SY

8) **магазин одягу** (clothing store)
ma-ha-ZYN O-d'a-hu

9) **дитяча ігрова кімната** (children's playroom)
dy-T'A-cha ih-ro-VA kim-NA-ta

10) **охоронець** (security guard)
o-kho-RO-nets'

11) **камера спостереження** (surveillance camera)
KA-me-ra spo-ste-RE-zhen'-n'a

12) **пекарня** (bakery)
pe-KAR-n'a

13) **магазин спорттоварів** (sports store)
ma-ha-ZYN sport-to-VA-riv

14) **фонтан** (fountain)
fon-TAN

Я працюю охоронцем у торговому центрі.
I work as a security guard in a mall.

Залишмо дітей в ігровій кімнаті!
Let's leave the kids in the playroom.

Мої родичі відкрили магазин одягу.
My relatives opened a clothing store.

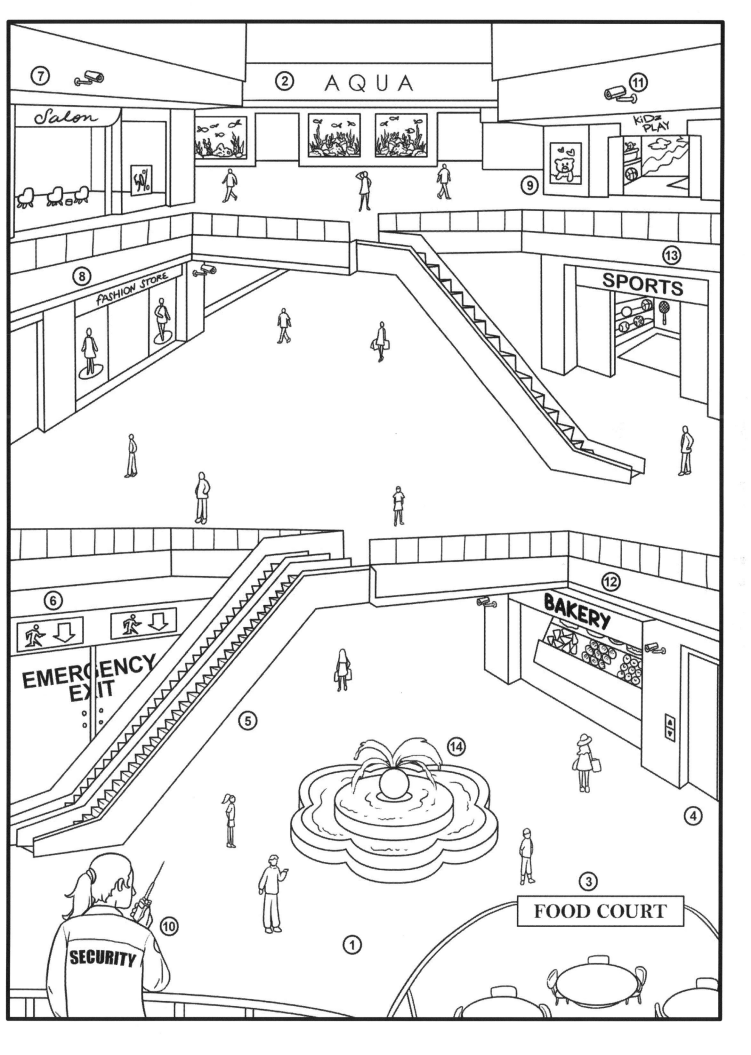

ДІЄСЛОВА I (VERBS I)

1) **розмовляти** (to talk)
   roz-mov-L'A-ty

2) **пити** (to drink)
   PY-ty

3) **їсти** (to eat)
   YIS-ty

4) **гуляти** (to walk)
   hu-L'A-ty

5) **відчинити** (to open)
   vid-chy-NY-ty

6) **зачинити** (to close)
   za-chy-NY-ty

7) **дати** (to give)
   DA-ty

8) **бачити** (to see)
   BA-chy-ty

9) **йти за** (to follow)
   jty za

10) **обіймати** (to hug)
    o-bij-MA-ty

11) **цілувати** (to kiss)
    tsi-lu-VA-ty

12) **купувати** (to buy)
    ku-pu-VA-ty

13) **слухати** (to listen)
    SLU-ha-ty

14) **співати** (to sing)
    spi-VA-ty

15) **танцювати** (to dance)
    tan-ts'u-VA-ty

Ми купуємо овочі на ринку.
We buy vegetables at the market.

Чому ти йдеш за мною?
Why are you following me?

Я взагалі не вмію співати.
I can't sing at all.

ДІЄСЛОВА ІІ (VERBS ІІ)

1) **писати** (to write)
py-SA-ty

2) **читати** (to read)
chy-TA-ty

3) **чистити** (to clean)
CHYS-ty-ty

4) **підіймати** (to pick up)
pi-dij-MA-ty

5) **знайти** (to find)
znaj-TY

6) **мити** (to wash)
MY-ty

7) **дивитися** (to watch)
dy-VY-ty-s'a

8) **ремонтувати** (to fix)
re-mon-tu-VA-ty

9) **думати** (to think)
DU-ma-ty

10) **брати** (to take)
BRA-ty

11) **різати** (to cut)
RI-za-ty

12) **зупинитися/припинити** (to stop)
zu-py-NY-ty-s'a/pry-py-NY-ty

13) **плакати** (to cry)
PLA-ka-ty

14) **посміхатися** (to smile)
po-smi-KHA-ty-s'a

15) **допомагати** (to help)
do-po-mo-HA-ty

Я люблю читати в метро.
I like reading on the subway.

Перед їжею треба мити руки.
One should wash hands before meals.

Припини скаржитися, будь ласка!
Please, stop complaining!

БУДІВНИЦТВО I (CONSTRUCTION I)

1) **кран** (crane)
kran

2) **сигнальна стрічка** (hazard tape)
syh-NAL'-na STRICH-ka

3) **дорожній конус** (traffic cone)
do-ROZH-nij KO-nus

4) **будівельна лопата** (construction shovel/spade)
bu-di-VEL'-na lo-PA-ta

5) **молоток** (hammer)
mo-lo-TOK

6) **різаки для дроту** (wire cutters)
ri-za-KY dl'a DRO-tu

7) **малярський валик** (paint roller)
ma-L'ARS'-kyj VA-lyk

8) **бензопила** (chainsaw)
ben-zo-py-LA

9) **дриль** (drill)
dryl'

10) **відбійний молоток** (jackhammer)
vid-BIJ-nyj mo-lo-TOK

11) **плоскогубці** (pliers)
plos-ko-HUB-tsi

12) **викрутка** (screwdriver)
VYK-rut-ka

Дай мені викрутку, будь ласка!
Give me the screwdriver, please.

Ми фарбували стіни малярським валиком.
We were painting the walls with a paint roller.

Цей молоток занадто важкий для мене.
This hammer is too heavy for me.

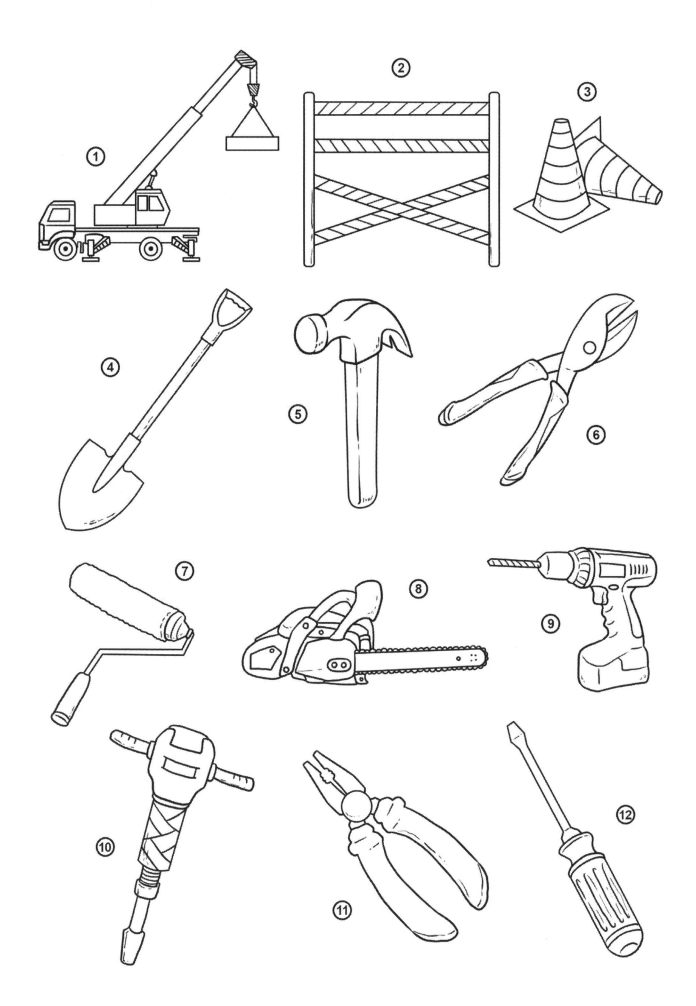

БУДІВНИЦТВО ІІ (CONSTRUCTION ІІ)

1) **ящик з інструментами** (toolbox)
   YA-schyk z ins-tru-MEN-ta-my

2) **каска** (helmet/hard hat)
   KAS-ka

3) **креслення** (blueprint)
   KRES-len'-n'a

4) **труби** (pipes)
   TRU-by

5) **шпатель** (trowel)
   SHPA-tel'

6) **бетономішалка** (concrete mixer)
   be-to-no-mi-SHAL-ka

7) **цегла/цеглини** (brick/bricks)
   TSEH-la/tseh-LY-ny

8) **будівельні матеріали** (building materials)
   bu-di-VEL'-ni ma-te-ri-A-ly

9) **плитка** (tiles)
   PLYT-ka

10) **цемент** (cement)
    tse-MENT

11) **пісок** (sand)
    pi-SOK

12) **гравій** (gravel)
    HRA-vij

Ці цеглини недорогі.
These bricks are inexpensive.

Ми купили нашому дідусеві ящик з інструментами.
We've bought a toolbox for our grandfather.

Нам не вистачає гравію для бетону.
We don't have enough gravel for the concrete.

QUIZ #7

Use arrows to match English words with their corresponding Ukrainian translations:

a. floor

b. near

c. subway

d. buy

e. open

f. wash

g. traffic police

h. starter

i. beauty salon

j. virtuous

k. outside

l. dinner

m. blueprint

n. follow

o. screwdriver

p. brick

1. креслення

2. поверх

3. купувати

4. викрутка

5. салон краси

6. ДАІ

7. біля/поруч

8. віртуозний

9. мити

10. вечеря

11. йти за

12. метро

13. відчинений

14. закуска

15. зовні

16. цегла

Fill in the blank spaces with the options below (use each word only once):

Мій день розпочався _____. Я працюю _____ в ресторані. Робота починається рано, а я далеко живу. Тому вранці я йду на _____. У мене був _____ настрій. На голові у мене були навушники, я йшла, _____ музику та _____. Тому я не помітила _____ плитку на тротуарі! Я наступила на неї і впала. Мені було дуже боляче, хотілося навіть _____. Я заспокоїлася, але день вже зіпсований!

автобусну зупинку   зламану

співала   погано

кухаркою   заплакати

добрий   слухала

РОСЛИНИ І ДЕРЕВА (PLANTS AND TREES)

1) **польова квітка** (wildflower)
po-l'o-VA KVIT-ka

2) **лікарська рослина** (medicinal plant)
LI-kars'-ka ros-LY-na

3) **гриб** (mushroom)
hryb

4) **бур'ян** (weed)
bur'-YAN

5) **морські водорості** (seaweed)
mors'-KI VO-do-ros-ti

6) **папороть** (fern)
PA-po-rot'

7) **очерет** (reed)
o-che-RET

8) **бамбук** (bamboo)
bam-BUK

9) **плющ** (ivy)
pl'usch

10) **мох** (moss)
moh

11) **трава** (grass)
tra-VA

12) **пальма** (palm tree)
PAL'-ma

13) **мангри** (mangrove)
MAN-hry

14) **кактус** (cactus)
KAK-tus

Бур'ян в саду зводить мене з розуму!
These weeds in the garden drive me mad!

Ці меблі виготовлені з бамбука.
This furniture is made of bamboo.

Влітку ми збираємо лікарські рослини.
We collect medicinal plants in summer.

КАРНАВАЛ (THE CARNIVAL)

1) **маска** (mask)
MAS-ka

2) **костюм/вбрання** (costume/outfit)
kos-T'UM/vbran'-N'A

3) **блазень** (harlequin)
BLA-zen'

4) **квіти** (flowers)
KVI-ty

5) **малий барабан** (snare drum)
MA-lyj ba-ra-BAN

6) **клоун** (clown)
KLO-un

7) **супергерой** (superhero)
su-per-he-ROJ

8) **принцеса** (princess)
pryn-TSE-sa

9) **космонавт** (astronaut)
kos-mo-NAVT

10) **мім** (mime)
mim

11) **в'язень/ув'язнений** (prisoner)
V'YA-zen'/u-V'YAZ-ne-nyj

12) **побутовий прилад** (household appliance)
po-bu-TO-vyj PRY-lad

13) **фея** (fairy)
FE-ya

14) **лісоруб** (lumberjack)
li-so-RUB

Моя донька вбралася феєю.
My daughter dressed up as a fairy.

Не всі клоуни смішні.
Not all clowns are funny.

Ув'язнений утік вночі.
The prisoner escaped at night.

МАЙСТЕРНЯ (THE WORKSHOP)

1) **інструмент** (tool)
ins-tru-MENT

2) **шорно-сідельні вироби** (saddlery)
SHOR-no si-DEL'-ni VY-ro-by

3) **столярні вироби/вироби з дерева**
(carpentry/woodwork)
sto-L'AR-ni VY-ro-by/VY-ro-by z
DE-re-va

4) **оббивка** (upholstery)
ob-BYV-ka

5) **чоботарство**
(shoemaking/shoe repair)
cho-bo-TARS-tvo

6) **ювелір** (jeweler)
yu-ve-LIR

7) **коваль** (blacksmith)
KO-val'

8) **механік** (mechanic)
me-KHA-nik

9) **текстильна промисловість**
(textile industry)
teks-TYL'-na pro-mys-LO-vist'

10) **пекарня** (bakery)
pe-KAR-n'a

11) **біжутерія** (costume jewelry)
bi-zhu-TE-ri-ya

12) **взуття** (footwear)
vzut-T'A

13) **обслуговування** (maintenance)
ob-slu-HO-vu-van'-n'a

14) **ремонт** (repair)
re-MONT

15) **живопис/малювання** (painting)
zhy-VO-pys/ma-l'u-VAN'-n'a

16) **тістечка/кондитерські вироби**
(pastry)
TIS-tech-ka/kon-DY-ters'-ki VY-ro-by

Він успадкував пекарню від батька.
He inherited the bakery from his father.

Ця біжутерія ручної роботи.
This costume jewelry is handmade.

Я займаюся живописом з п'яти років.
I've been painting since I was five.

ПРОДУКТОВИЙ МАГАЗИН (THE GROCERY STORE)

1) **паста** (pasta)
PAS-ta

2) **рис** (rice)
rys

3) **вівсяні пластівці/вівсянка** (oats)
viv-S'A-ni plas-tiv-TSI/viv-S'AN-ka

4) **хліб** (bread)
khlib

5) **олії** (oils)
o-LI-yi

6) **соуси** (sauces)
SO-u-sy

7) **заправки для салатів** (salad dressings)
zap-RAV-ky dl'a sa-LA-tiv

8) **приправи** (condiments)
pryp-RA-vy

9) **консерви** (canned goods)
kon-SER-vy

10) **шинка** (ham)
SCHYN-ka

11) **сир** (cheese)
syr

12) **арахісове масло** (peanut butter)
a-RA-khi-so-ve MAS-lo

13) **цукерки** (candy)
tsu-KER-ky

14) **боби** (beans)
bo-BY

15) **кава** (coffee)
KA-va

16) **чай** (tea)
chaj

Як можна їсти вівсянку щоранку?
How can one eat oats every morning?

Ці приправи занадто гострі.
These condiments are too spicy.

Це шоколадні цукерки?
Are these candies chocolate ones?

ПОДОРОЖІ I (TRAVEL AND LIVING I)

1) **хазяїн m./хазяйка f.** (host)
ha-Z'A-yin/ ha-Z'AJ-ka

2) **турист m./туристка f.** (tourist)
tu-RYST/tu-RYST-ka

3) **мандрівник m./ мандрівниця f.** (traveler)
man-driv-NYK/man-driv-NY-ts'a

4) **багаж** (luggage)
ba-HAZH

5) **ручна поклажа** (hand luggage)
ruch-NA pok-LA-zha

6) **фотоаппарат** (camera)
fo-to-ap-pa-RAT

7) **готель** (hotel)
ho-TEL'

8) **хостел** (hostel)
HOS-tel

9) **постоялий двір** (inn)
pos-to-YA-lyj dvir

10) **хатина** (cabin)
ha-TY-na

11) **намет** (tent)
na-MET

12) **авіарейс** (flight)
a-vi-a-REJS

13) **відправлення** (departure)
vid-PRAV-len'-n'a

14) **прибуття** (arrival)
pry-but'-T'A

Я не пам'ятаю, о котрій годині ти прибуваєш.
I don't remember your arrival time.

Вона взяла інтерв'ю у відомого мандрівника.
She interviewed a famous traveler.

Ми маємо хатинку в лісі.
We've got a cabin in the woods.

ПОДОРОЖІ II (TRAVEL AND LIVING II)

1) **місто** (town)
MIS-to

2) **карта** (map)
KAR-ta

3) **автобусна зупинка** (bus stop)
av-TO-bus-na zu-PYN-ka

4) **таксі** (taxi)
tak-SI

5) **прокат автомобілів** (car rental)
pro-KAT av-to-mo-BI-liv

6) **залізнична станція** (train station)
za-liz-NYCH-na STAN-tsi-ya

7) **аеропорт** (airport)
a-e-ro-PORT

8) **паспорт** (passport)
PAS-port

9) **посвідчення особи**
(ID/identification card)
po-SVID-chen'-n'a o-SO-by

10) **валюта** (currency)
va-L'U-ta

11) **готівка** (cash)
ho-TIV-ka

12) **дебетова картка** (debit card)
de-be-TO-va KART-ka

13) **кредитна картка** (credit card)
kre-DYT-na KART-ka

14) **екскурсовод** (tourist guide)
eks-kur-so-VOD

Яка валюта в цій країні?
What currency do they use in this country?

У тебе є карта міста?
Do you have the city map?

Я заплачу готівкою.
I'm paying in cash.

ІГРАШКИ (TOYS)

1) **м'яч** (ball)
   m'yach

2) **плюшевий ведмедик** (teddy bear)
   PL'U-she-vyj ved-ME-dyk

3) **поїзд** (train)
   PO-yizd

4) **скейтборд** (skateboard)
   SKEJT-bord

5) **лялька** (doll)
   L'AL'-ka

6) **перегоновий автомобіль** (race car)
   pe-re-HO-no-vyj av-to-mo-BIL'

7) **робот** (robot)
   RO-bot

8) **повітряний змій** (kite)
   po-VIT-r'a-nyj zmij

9) **барабан** (drum)
   ba-ra-BAN

10) **хула-хуп** (hula hoop)
    hu-la-HUP

11) **візок** (wagon)
    vi-ZOK

12) **фігурки** (blocks)
    fi-HUR-ky

13) **ксилофон** (xylophone)
    ksy-lo-FON

14) **вантажівка** (truck)
    van-ta-ZHIV-ka

15) **літак** (airplane)
    li-TAK

16) **дитячі кубики** (blocks)
    dy-T'A-chi KU-by-ky

Скільки в тебе ляльок?
How many dolls do you have?

На день народження мені подарували робота.
I got a robot for my birthday.

Давай запустимо повітряного змія!
Let's fly a kite!

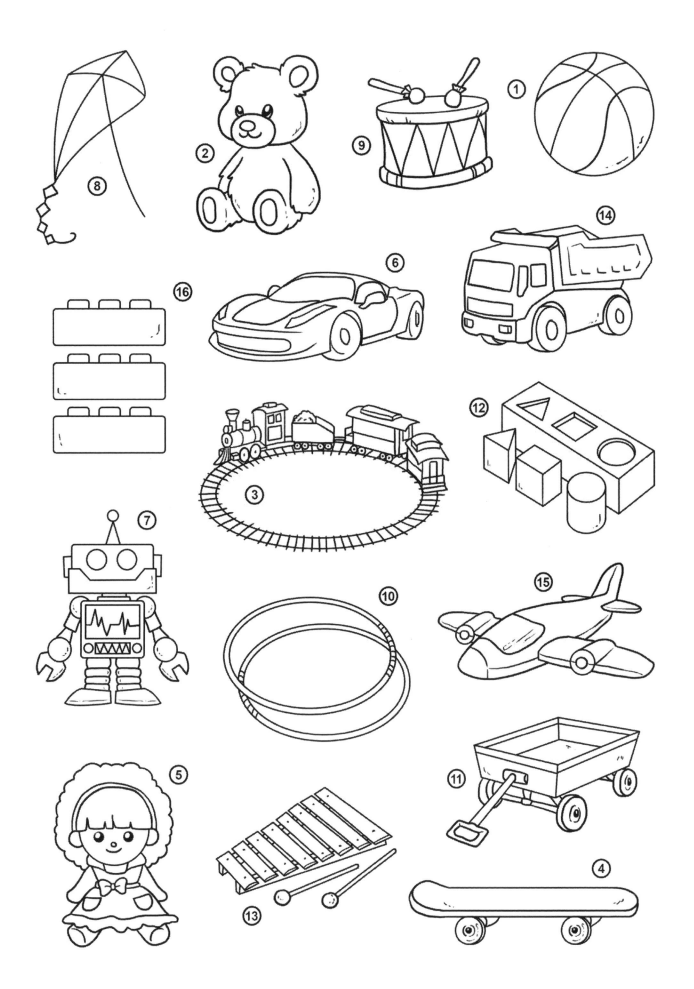

ДЕНЬ НАРОДЖЕННЯ (THE BIRTHDAY PARTY)

1) **плакат на день народження**
(birthday banner)
pla-KAT na den' na-ROD-zhen'-n'a

2) **прикраси** (decorations)
pry-KRA-sy

3) **подарунок** (present/gift)
po-da-RU-nok

4) **столові прибори** (cutlery)
sto-LO-vi pry-BO-ry

5) **іменинник m./іменинниця f.)**
(birthday person)
i-me-NYN-nyk/i-me-NYN-ny-ts'a

6) **повітряні кульки** (balloons)
po-VIT-r'a-ni KUL'ky

7) **святковий торт** (birthday cake)
sv'at-KO-vyj tort

8) **тарілки** (plates)
ta-ril-KY

9) **виделки** (forks)
vy-DEL-ky

10) **ложки** (spoons)
LOZH-ky

11) **чашки** (cups)
chash-KY

12) **соломинка** (straw)
so-lo-MYN-ka

13) **піньята** (piñata)
pin'-YA-ta

14) **свічка** (candle)
SVICH-ka

15) **ковпак** (hat)
kov-PAK

16) **гості** (guests)
HOS-ti

Хто тут іменинник?
Who is the birthday person here?

Я купила паперові тарілки для вечірки.
I've bought paper plates for the party.

Дивися, скільки тут повітряних кульок!
Look how many balloons there are!

АНТОНІМИ (ANTONYMS)

1) **чистий** (clean)
CHYS-tyj

2) **брудний** (dirty)
brud-NYJ

3) **мало** (few)
MA-lo

4) **багато** (many)
ba-HA-to

5) **нападати** (attack)
na-pa-DA-ty

6) **захищатися** (defend)
za-khy-SCHA-ty-s'a

7) **прямий** (straight)
pr'a-MYJ

8) **вигнутий** (curved)
VYH-nu-tyj

9) **разом** (together)
ra-ZOM

10) **в розлуці** (separated)
v roz-LU-tsi

11) **молодий** (young)
mo-lo-DYJ

12) **старий** (old)
sta-RYJ

13) **багатство** (wealth)
ba-HAT-stvo

14) **бідність** (poverty)
BID'-nist'

15) **увігнутий** (concave)
u-VIH-nu-tyj

16) **опуклий** (convex)
o-PUK-lyj

Ми ніколи не будемо разом.
We will never be together.

У тебе багато друзів?
Do you have many friends?

Я вже не молодий.
I'm not young anymore.

QUIZ #8

Use arrows to match English words with their corresponding Ukrainian translations:

a. grass

b. pastry

c. tea

d. flowers

e. cheese

f. cash

g. seaweed

h. tent

i. footwear

j. drum

k. lumberjack

l. doll

m. luggage

n. decorations

o. map

p. wealth

1. барабан

2. квіти

3. багатство

4. трава

5. лялька

6. карта

7. намет

8. сир

9. взуття

10. тістечка

11. лісоруб

12. прикраси

13. готівка

14. чай

15. багаж

16. морські водорості

Fill in the blank spaces with the options below (use each word only once):

Ми з чоловіком зараз у відпустці. Ми відпочиваємо в маленькому _____ біля моря. Ми приїхали сюди _____ і зупинилися в приватному готелі. Він не новий, навпаки, дуже _____, але _____ та акуратний. Тут дуже смачно готують _____, лазанью та пасту. Але більш за все мені подобається _____. Тут навіть роблять _____ ручної роботи. Ми купили їх для своїх друзів та родичів. _____ готелю – добрий чоловік похилого віку. Приймати _____ – це його бізнес, але раніше він працював _____.

Це старе місто і тут багато цікавого. _____ розповів нам історію міста. У нас чудова відпустка, але через пандемію ми всюди носимо _____.

старий   гриби

господар   місті

випічка   гостей

поїздом   цукерки

екскурсовод   чистий

маски   ювеліром

CONCLUSION

While there is certainly much more to say about the Ukrainian language, we hope that this general overview will help you understand and use the vocabulary from this dictionary, and your own vocabulary, as you continue your journey to bilingualism.

We would like to leave you with a few suggestions for a pleasant and fruitful language learning experience:

1. Learn what you need and what you love.

    While survival Ukrainian is indispensable, mechanical memorization of long lists of words is not the best use of your time and energy. Make sure to focus on the vocabulary that is important and useful in your life. Perhaps you need Ukrainian for work or to visit family and friends. In this case, make sure that you concentrate on the phrases that will be help you reach these goals.

2. Do not skip learning grammar and tenses.

    Although it is not the most exciting part of learning a language, spending some time perfecting your grammar is the key to being able to manipulate the language in the long term.

3. Use available media to practice all aspects of the language.

    Movies, music, and social media provide the opportunity to practice reading, writing, and listening at any time from your phone or laptop. Aim to spend twenty minutes a day on the Ukrainian language in order to make good progress.

4. Practice speaking as soon as you can with a native speaker.

    You can join speaking groups in real life or online.

5. Remember: **Communication before perfection**.

    It takes years to master a language, and fluency is not achieved easily. It requires commitment and regular practice. However, if you get to visit Ukraine, do not hesitate to try to speak Ukrainian with everyone you meet. This will give you the motivation and confidence to carry on learning. You might feel scared at first, but do not worry. People will be kind to you!

6. Enjoy the journey!

ANSWERS

QUIZ #1

a-8.   b-10.   c-16.   d-1.   e-14.   f-2.   g-11.   h-3.   i-7.   j-13.   k-5.   l-15.
m-4.   n-9.   o-6.   p-12.

Маленький Матвій сьогодні **сумний**. Він плаче, його обличчя та **очі** червоні від сліз. **Бабуся** обіцяла відвести його до зоопарку. Матвій обожнює тварин. У нього є кролик, ігуана та **хом'як**. Але вони не можуть поїхати до зоопарку, бо автомобіль зламався. «Матвію, не плач, – просить бабуся, - ти краєш мені **серце**. Ти мій улюблений внук, але я не можу полагодити автомобіль сама!» Матвій розуміє, але не може заспокоїтись. Віктор Іванович – **сусід** бабусі. Він пропонує відвезти їх до зоопарку своїм автомобілем. Тепер Матвій **щасливий**. Він побачив бегемота, жирафа, гепарда і навіть **лева**! З птахів йому дуже сподобалися ара та **ківі**.

«Дякую, – каже бабуся, – ваша **доброта** врятувала мого внука!

–Нема за що, – відповідає Віктор Іванович, – щаслива дитина – це найкраща **подяка**».

QUIZ #2

a-14.   b-11.   c-1.   d-13.   e-12.   f-4.   g-10.   h-7.   i-15.   j-3.   k-16.   l-8.
m-5.   n-9.   o-6.   p-2.

Цих вихідних мої друзі хочуть **жити в наметах**. Вони кажуть, що буде весело. Але мені не подобається ця ідея. Намети – це дискомфорт. Потрібно брати шорти, джинси, плащі, а я люблю сукні та **спідниці**. Буде сонячно та спекотно, а я не люблю таку погоду. Я люблю, коли **прохолодно**. Так, там є **озеро**, але я не люблю плавати. Я можу засмагати, якщо є **сонцезахисний крем**, але недовго. Окрім того, я боюся комах: ґедзів, мух, **комарів**! А дикі тварини? Кажани і **вовки**! Ще мої друзі будуть їсти **рибу** з озера. Але я не люблю рибу! Напевно, я залишуся вдома.

QUIZ #3

a-5. b-7. c-12. d-1. e-14. f-4. g-2. h-16. i-13. j-9. k-10. l-3.
m-11. n-8. o-6 p-15.

Цей рік найщасливіший у моєму житті: ми купили будинок! Ми переїжджаємо через **два тижні**. Біля будинку є великий **гараж** для нашого автомобіля. Перед будинком – великий **ґанок**. Тут я буду вкриватися вовняним пледом і читати книги. Відчинимо **двері**? Велика вітальня, мені дуже подобається диван та **камін**. І, звичайно ж, **книжкова полиця** для моїх книг! У кухні є велика **комора** і духовка. Тут я буду пекти **імбирне печиво**. У їдальні – великий та широкий **обідній стіл**, якраз для нашої родини. У спальні є ліжко та **комод**, але він маленький для моїх речей. У ванній кімнаті є **душ,** але немає ванни. Я дуже щаслива і не можу дочекатися переїзду!

QUIZ #4

a-2. b-6. c-15. d-16. e-7. f-1. g-10. h-13. i-5. j-9. k-3. l-11.
m-14. n-12. o-8. p-4.

Мені 17 років. Прощавай, школо, прощавай, **шкільна парто!** Потрібно вибрати професію. **Дід Мороз** залишив під ялинкою великий гарний блокнот. Я беру блокнот, **ручку** і записую професії. Мені подобається спорт, особливо **боротьба**, але я не хочу займатися цим професійно. Може, фотограф? Я подорожуватиму і фотографуватиму пейзажі: водоспади, пустелі та **вулкани**. Або я стану **пожежником**! Хоча ні, це небезпечно. Я буду **бізнесменом**! Я сидітиму в офісі, і в мене буде багато працівників. Але офіс це нудно: комп'ютер, принтер, **папки**. Ні, бізнес не для мене. А, може, я буду пілотом? Але я боюся **літаків**! Знаю! Я куплю **повітряну кулю** і полечу у подорож. Але я обіцяв допомогти мамі. У саду на мене чекає **газонокосарка**, а потім відро та **швабра**. До зустрічі, блокноте!

QUIZ #5

a-5. b-11. c-2 d-8. e-12. f-3. g-9. h-13. i-4. j-16. k-15. l-7.
m-10. n-1. o-14. p-6.

Я **вчений** і працюю в лабораторії. Мої друзі фермери і мешкають на **сході** країни. Вони запросили мене у гості, і я з радістю погодився! Жодних комп'ютерів, веб-камер та інших **приладів**. Лише свіже повітря, природа, корови і **кури**. А ще мої друзі вирощують овочі: картоплю, гарбузи та **помідори**. Я купив екзотичні фрукти: папайю та **ананас**. Ми зустрілися, пообідали, і мої друзі пішли доїти корів. Я хотів їм допомогти, але корова вдарила мене копитом прямо по голові! Я подумав, що це **затемнення**! В очах стало темно. Мої друзі викликали **швидку**. Лікар сказав, що

193

все добре. Увечері ми сиділи на ганку і дивилися на **місяць**. Мій друг грав на **гітарі**, і я забув про випадок із коровою.

QUIZ #6

a-6.　b-12.　c-1.　d-15.　e-9.　f-14.　g-16.　h-10.　i-7.　j-2.　k-11.　l-8.
m-5.　n-3.　o-13.　p-4.

Сьогодні свято – мій **день народження**. Я не хотів гучного свята, просто **тихого** вечора вдома. Я замовив устриць та **лобстера** і хотів просто сидіти вдома та дивитися **фільм**. Але зранку прийшли мої батьки. Тато подарував мені **мобільний телефон**, а мама спекла розкішний **десерт** – торт у формі **серця** з родзинками та **волоськими горіхами**. Ще вона приготувала мій улюблений **м'ясний рулет**.

Потім прийшли мої друзі, і ми пішли до парку розваг. Ми каталися на **колесі огляду**, їли **цукрову вату** і розважалися на **гральних автоматах**. Це був чудовий день народження! Краще, ніж сидіти вдома та дивитися фільм!

QUIZ #7

a-2.　b-7.　c-12.　d-3.　e-13.　f-9.　g-6.　h-14.　i-5.　j-8.　k-15.　l-10.
m-1.　n-11.　o-4.　p-16.

Мій день розпочався **погано**. Я працюю **кухаркою** в ресторані. Робота починається рано, а я далеко живу. Тому вранці я йду на **автобусну зупинку**. У мене був **добрий** настрій. На голові у мене були навушники, я йшла, **слухала** музику та **співала**. Тому я не помітила **зламану** плитку на тротуарі! Я наступила на неї і впала. Мені було дуже боляче, хотілося навіть **заплакати**. Я заспокоїлася, але день вже зіпсований!

QUIZ #8

a-4.　b-10.　c-14.　d-2.　e-8.　f-13.　g-16.　h-7.　i-9.　j-1.　k-11.　l-5.
m-15.　n-12.　o-6.　p-3.

Ми з чоловіком зараз у відпустці. Ми відпочиваємо в маленькому **місті** біля моря. Ми приїхали сюди **поїздом** і зупинилися в приватному готелі. Він не новий, навпаки, дуже **старий**, але **чистий** та акуратний. Тут дуже смачно готують **гриби**, лазанью та пасту. Але більш за все мені подобається **випічка**. Тут навіть роблять **цукерки** ручної роботи. Ми купили їх для своїх друзів та родичів.

Господар готелю – добрий чоловік похилого віку. Приймати **гостей** - це його бізнес, але раніше він працював **ювеліром**.

Це старе місто і тут багато цікавого. **Екскурсовод** розповів нам історію міста. У нас чудова відпустка, але через пандемію ми всюди носимо **маски**.

Printed in Great Britain
by Amazon